Radical Tarot

Breaking all the Rules

Vincent Pitisci

Radical Tarot - Breaking all the Rules   Copyright © 2017 by Vincent Pitisci

Illustrations from the Universal Waite Tarot Deck® reproduced by permission of U.S. Games Systems, Inc., Stamford, CT 06902 USA. Copyright ©1990 by U.S. Games Systems, Inc. Further reproduction prohibited. The Universal Waite Tarot Deck® is a registered trademark of U.S. Games Systems, Inc.

Illustrations from the IJJ Swiss Tarot Deck® reproduced by permission of U.S. Games Systems, Inc., Stamford, CT 06902 USA. Copyright ©1970 by U.S. Games Systems, Inc. Further reproduction prohibited. The IJJ Swiss Tarot Deck® is a registered trademark of U.S. Games Systems, Inc.

All rights reserved. No part of this book may be reproduced in any form, except brief excerpts for purpose of review without written permission from the author.

CreateSpace Independent Publishing Platform

Dedication

To all of those I've ever had the pleasure to read....to teach....to work with.
You have helped me on my journey as much as I've helped you on your's.

I hope you don't mind......
I hope you don't mind......

That I put down in words........

How wonderful life is while you're in the world

~ Elton John

Contents

Acknowledgments

Preface – A Day at the Fair 9

Introduction 15

Chapter 1. Tarot Card Readings are a
Creative Thinking Technique 19

Chapter 2. Conceptual Blending & Tarot Cards 27

Chapter 3. The Importance of Randomness 33

Chapter 4. Finding Meaning in the Cards 41

Chapter 5. Working a Card Spread 127

Chapter 6. Other Fancy Stuff 163

Chapter 7. Conversations with the Tarot 173

ACKNOWLEDGEMENTS

I would like to acknowledge creative thinker Michael Michalko who's knowledge and talent in explaining creative thinking allowed me to see the connection.
His books *THINKERTOYS – a handbook of creative thinking techniques, CRACKING CREATIVITY – The Secrets of Creative Genius, CREATIVE THINKERING – Putting Your Imagination to Work THINKPAK – a brainstorming card deck* was how I was able to connect-the-dots to crack open this centuries old mystery. It was his easy flowing insight that allowed me to see what has never been seen before.

I would also like to acknowledge Michael J. Gelb for his insight on my journey with his book *HOW TO THINK LIKE LEONARDO da VINCI Seven Steps to Genius Everyday,*

The work from you both has guided me to seeing new insight to a very old mystery that has never been seen before.

Preface

A Day at the Fair

There are many scenarios to being a professional card reader. I enjoy them all but annual fairs and festivals bring about an energy that does something to you. A hundred vendors all selling their wares. The sight of a carnival's Ferris wheel on one end of the midway and a food court at the other. Beer gardens and sound stages here and there throughout.

And you're somewhere in the middle of it all. The afternoons drift along at a casual pace and the nights flow into movement of colored lights mixed with the constant hum of happy voices all around you. And there you are, sharing the experience with a number of other readers in a 30-foot tent outlined by long tables with folding chairs on all sides.

We do a few annual fairs. There are usually about 15 readers and we gather every year. The fairs last from Thursday till Sunday. Noon till midnight each day. Four straight 12-hour days.

We all meet on Thursday morning and discuss what has being going on all year as we exchange new stories and reminisce old ones. We are the readers. The day starts around 11am with us setting up our table arrangements and having a few laughs as we sip on coffee from the cafe vendor right across the midway.

At 12:00 the fair opens its gates to the public and a small crowd of curious people enter onto the fair grounds. A few come to our tent but the day will be slow and easy until later on. The pace picks up around 3pm. By then most of us have had two or three readings under our belt with the crowd picking up at a steady pace as the clock ticks on and the afternoon moves along easily.

Around 6pm people leaving work are filing into the fair grounds. The beer gardens are half full and people are working on the sound stages nearby making ready for the bands that will play tonight. The crowd coming to our tent is steadily increasing and we are starting to get busy with less small talk and more readings.

By 8pm the midway is filling up and we are spending most of the hour reading clients. Voices are heard from all directions and every reader is throwing cards. Every now and then you will hear loud humming coming from instruments tuning up from the sound stage and the beer gardens are busy and happy. Many people walk by with curiosity. Some stop, some walk on to the next tent and the buzz of the fair is in high gear.

By 9pm all of us have been reading steady. One after the other. The beer garden is going full tilt and the stage nearby has a band playing strong.

The lights are turned on within the tent as the warmer sunshine of the day is replaced with the cooler breezes of the night. We are no longer able to converse with each other at all as we are too busy reading seekers of the future. The colored lights from every direction and various activities around you are increasing steadily as the night moves along.

By 10pm the pace is full throttle. Every reader has their table occupied with two or three others waiting in line. The peoples energy shifts from quietly curious to talkative and friendly. All are chatting with each other as they wait in line for their turn, sipping on wine or beer from plastic glasses.

No matter how much water you drink, your throat is dry from talking over the loud music coming from the sound stage.

You've been here for 10 hours and the folding chair you're sitting on feels like it's sinking into the ground. The day is getting long. But the pace is so quick you don't give it too much thought. You're busy watching the clients closely as they sit with you, making sure they don't tip over their wine glass onto your cards as they explain their questions using their hands in a very friendly manner – as if they have known you for years.

By 11pm the readings have been full throttle with a crowd waiting four deep to see you. Noise and confusion. "Who's next?! HELLO!" You look at the next person in line and point to your table. As she sits down you yell out with a raspy voice over all the noise – "CUT THE CARDS!" Comments are yelled out from a crowd of her friends nearby as she sits across from you. "DON'T FORGET TO ASK HIM ABOUT TOM! THIS IS GONNA BE GOOD!" — "HEY, ARE YOU REALLY PSYCHIC? COME ON, TELL ME SOMETHING I KNOW. PROVE IT. HA HA HA!"

Then they all listen in as you speak over the band which is too loud from the nearby stage. The constant rattle of ice cubes, the murmur of voices coming from every direction, the loud music and your own words fill your head with mixed thoughts like a roller coaster ride. And you read. Even the cards images seem to be a little distracted by the surroundings.

You gotta use the bathroom but if you stand up a whole crowd of waiting clients yell out "HEY! WHERE YOU GOING?! COME ON!" By now the line to see you is five deep. You keep turning cards and you read.

At 11:45 you feel as though your mind has gone blank. You point to the last reading to sit and tell the rest "She's the last one"
They all complain. "I'VE BEEN STANDING HERE WAITING AND YOU GONNA TELL ME YOU WON'T READ ME!!??"
"That's right– She's the last." She looks back at her friends as if to say *HaHa* as she sits across from you.

The cards seem to be looking back at you as if to say *'I'm out of meanings. You're running on empty.'* As you look at her you think – one last reading. She seems nice and has been waiting a long time to see you. As you finish the reading you think.... I'm done. She throws you a $5 tip and says "Thank you Vincent."

You start to pack it up. The lights are turning off in the fairgrounds. People start walking towards the exits. You didn't even notice that the band has stopped playing. The quiet is nice. The whole mood changes quickly. You turn around to the other readers. They look just as tired as you and even the tent itself seems to give out a sigh of relief.

The change-makers start exchanging our tickets for money. How many did you do? I did 25 readings. I did 23. I did 19. I did 28. A good night!

Everyone is beat but feeling good about a busy day. One day done and three to go. Talking with each other as we pack up our gear, we make sure we have everything. Did I pack my timer? Yes, third pocket on my bag. Where's my cell phone? Car keys are here somewhere.

We walk to our cars around 1am with a pocket full of $20s through a dark empty parking lot. The fair grounds are quiet except for a few stragglers. We stay together making sure everyone gets to their car without being approached.

Lynda and I stop off at *Denny's* for a bite before going to our room at the *Motel-6* right next door. We eat and talk about how good it was to see Cathy. David looked good. I'm glad Brenda made it again this year. She's a good reader. I had one kook sit down for a reading but over all it was a good crowd. Had a couple of repeats from last year. Was good to see them.

Not a bad first night. Might have some rain tomorrow but Saturday and Sunday look clear. Should be a good fair.

We leave *Denny's* and walk over to our room. We sit with a glass of wine and count our money. "A good night. We did it again. Set a wake up call for 9am. I gotta get gas in the morning and I'm gonna want a good breakfast before we start again tomorrow."

You look at your deck of cards and feel they are as tired as you.
They really got a workout today. A true test.

We go to bed and as I lay there in the dark I can still hear the sounds of the fair in my mind. I find myself trying to make out the conversations of the people still talking in my head. The band is playing. The murmur of voices all around me. As I lie there listening, I drift off into sleep. Tomorrow me and those cards will sit another 12 hours with the others and do it all over again.

That's when you really feel it.......You're a Tarot card reader.

That was so beautiful

And now for the good stuff!

Introduction

Most things evolve over time. The more we understand something, the more we advance in its methods and applications. The Tarot cards are one of the few things that haven't taken this route. This is because we haven't been able to explain why Tarot cards work.

Why do they work? That has been the biggest mystery of the Tarot. How can a deck of mysterious cards predict our future? How can it show us answers not seen before? Now, after centuries of mystery – this missing cog in the wheel can be explained.

Today cognitive science would identify this centuries old mystery as a widely used creative thinking technique. Specifically, a creative thinking technique known as Conceptual Blending.

This same application is used today by creative consultants in science, medicine, the arts, advertising, and many other branches of society. It is used by authors, artists, inventors and other creative thinkers.

Creative consultants are sought out just like the Tarot card reader; for the same purpose. To find answers. Specific answers to questions being looked into. Questions being looked into for the future. In other words, to make a prediction. The Tarot cards are used in the same fashion and for the same purpose. To make a prediction.

Today the Tarot card reading's success can be seen as a creative thinking technique. In fact, you cannot do a Tarot card reading without using these same exact applications that today would be defined as creative thinking techniques. A deliberate creative thinking technique that in 1993 cognitive science has officially identified and given the term of Conceptual Blending.

Conceptual Blending is a thinking technique that combines two dissimilar concepts and creates associations between them to spark new ideas and insight to a question being looked into.

Placing a Tarot card into an element of a question we call a position in a card spread and making associations between the two to get a new idea would be defined today by cognitive science as the same creative thinking process. A creative thinking process that today we understand and is widely used.

One mind-set is based on cognitive science and the other is based on a centuries old pack of cards that see into the future. But they are the same set of thinking procedures. This new insight will explain why the Tarot card reading has been so effective over time. It explains why it works so well in finding answers not previously seen.

This new understanding will open up a whole new constellation of ideas and possibilities with the Tarot. Once we see why something works it allows us to improve it. To look into it deeper. It allows us to structure new applications and techniques never seen before or thought possible.

Taking the mystery out of the Tarot cards opens up doors to new mystery. New perceptions and understanding of what it is we are doing when we read these curious cards called the Tarot. It also helps us focus on the real source of insight these cards bring out in a reading. Our mind's ability to "see" new ideas.

Once you understand this mystery you will see the Tarot in a whole new light. You will also be able to use the Tarot with more effective results than before. More effective results than anyone ever has. Why? Because now you will not only know how to use Tarot cards, but for the first time in their history, you will know why they work.

Since the 1950s, psychology has been studying the way creative genius minds work. What has been found is deliberate applications of thought that create innovative ideas. Ideas that cannot be found through conventional thinking patterns and applications.

A way of thought that comes naturally to us all if we apply it. Now we know how it is done. It is a natural process that we can initiate at will. We use this process every time we do a Tarot card reading.

Understanding this opens up the capabilities with Tarot cards in immeasurable ways. It puts us at a place where we see we are just scratching the surface to the capabilities a Tarot reading can have.

For centuries, the Tarot's reputation has been labeled as mysterious. But now we can see that as all smoke and mirrors. A literal house-of-cards.

The strong mind-set of the Tarot cards being mysterious is centuries old. But if the Tarot cards came out today instead of centuries ago, they would not be viewed as mysterious at all.

They would be looked at as a common creative thinking technique used by more than just card readers. A technique that goes beyond a deck of 78 cards. A technique that deliberately taps into our mind's imagination and intuitive insight.

A creative thinking technique used by writers, inventors, artists, advertising agencies, Fortune 500 companies, the CIA, NASA, the Pentagon and other branches of our government, universities and many other places. Why? Because it works.

So, if you already read Tarot cards, pat yourself on the back, because what you've been doing all along is learning how to think like a genius.

It might be time for a change in the way we understand this unique and ingenious pack of cards.

And now this mad-hatter invites you to step through the looking glass to another Tarot tea-party

Hello... Legend has it that the spirit of an evil chicken roams the pages of this chapter.
That's right.... a Poultrygeist.

1. Tarot Card Readings are a Creative Thinking Technique

They say your future can be seen in the Tarot cards. I would rather think that your answers can be found in the Tarot cards. But only if they are used correctly. To use them correctly you need a technique. A system to find answers. And we have that in place. We call it a card reading. A card reading uses a card spread to look into a particular question asked. A card spread is a collection of assumptions that are meant to pertain to the question being looked into. Things that directly affect the question. A card spread is your question broken apart into segments like chapters of a book.

The other parts of the process seem vague and inconsistent from one source to another. Different card interpretations and different ways of doing various spreads all seem to fan out in many different directions of thought. But the techniques still give good results regardless of those inconsistencies. The cards do seem to work. Many have claimed to see that happen first hand.

And when we look into why this works – we always come up against a brick wall. Only vague answers or weak theories are found. Nothing that could be verified or confirmed from any viable source. No one could ever explain that part of the technique. No one could explain that part of the Tarot. And we have accepted that with no further thought.

Eden Gray had this to say about it in her book "The Complete Guide To The Tarot" 1970. *"In some way that we do not understand, your subconscious mind seems to direct the shuffling, but can do this correctly only after you have implanted the meaning of each card in your memory."*

But that classic book was written almost 50 years ago.

With today's understanding of the mind, we can explain it with logic and reason. We know more about the mind today than we did when I first picked up Tarot cards in 1969.

In his classic book *Tarot of the Bohemians* — 1889 *Papus* states in his preface — *"The Key to its construction and application has not yet been revealed, so far as I know."*

Then *Papus* went on to write a 350-page treatise on the subject. That is difficult to do when you don't know the construction or application of what it is you are writing about.

But that classic work was written at a time when secrecy was common and sources of information were scarce. Today we have so much more information at our finger tips. Breakthroughs of discovery are moving at a record pace on many subjects. A pace mankind has never seen before. Now we can see how things are connected in our world in ways we could never see before. How one thing works the same as another. This is how many breakthroughs and discoveries are found. Relating something we do understand – to something we do not.

The application of a Tarot card reading can now be seen from a different angle. A fairly recent study of a creative thinking technique. Specifically a technique known today as Conceptual Blending.

The mind-set of Tarot cards being able to mysteriously "see into your future" is centuries old. But now we can see this deck of cards for what it has always been – an imaginative and intuitive tool that allows us to see what we didn't see before.

The application of positions to a card spread and Tarot cards randomly placed into those positions are designed to create a pattern of thought that can break you out of your typical way of thinking. Your typical way of thinking is where old ideas remain stuck and keep repeating themselves in your head as dead-end solutions.

Creative thinking techniques break us out of that mode to create a way of thinking that cannot be achieved with conventional thought.

The Creative Thinking Procedure and the Tarot Card Reading:

A question broken apart into segments:
It is a universal tendency to fragment a subject into separate parts. The method for any logical analysis requires doing this.

All card spreads do this. We call the separate parts of the question – card spread positions.

Adding randomness into sections of our question to stimulate ideas:
Adding a randomness of some type to those separate parts of our question forces us to make a connection – an association not seen before. These associations will usually be made metaphorically to spark ideas. This technique forces us to see things we didn't see before. This is commonly known as adding a random stimulus to a question for new ideas.

Adding a random stimulus is a common technique used by creative consultants, think-tanks and other creative thinkers looking to find an answer not previously seen.

Associating and interpreting a random Tarot card to elements of our question known as card spread positions is how all Tarot card readings are done.

Who uses this application of thought today?
Scholarly interest in creative thinking is recognized by engineering, psychology, cognitive science, education, philosophy, technology, sociology, linguistics, business studies, song writing, comedy writing, economics and many other disciplines.

It is also something the centuries old Tarot card reader has been unknowingly practicing all along.

A deliberate, structured application of thought to stir new and innovative ideas, solve problems and answer questions. Questions for things to be done in the future.

In other words...to predict.

What does this mean?

For centuries the Tarot has been considered an unexplainable source of information. Now that source can be explained. With this new understanding of why the Tarot works it can be refined and improved for the first time in its history.

Without clearly understanding why the process works we have been forced to mimic applications from the past. We have been forced to use paint-by-numbers procedures when using these cards. Why? Because we didn't understand completely what it is we were doing.

If you can't explain why something works you can't refine it. You can't improve it. You can't make the process more effective.

Now we can see that the success of a card reading has never been in the cards themselves. It has been in the application they are used with. An application of thought that cannot be accomplished with conventional thinking.

Over the years we have seen the Tarot cards themselves evolve through beautiful artwork. But little has been done to improve the application. We still look at the application of card spreads with the same basic attitude and procedures we did centuries ago.

But now we can see that the success of a reading isn't coming from any magic in the Tarot cards themselves. It is coming from the way we look at a question. The application the cards are used in is what finds answers.

The cards help spark ideas of thought into whatever it is we're looking into. But the application of a card spread is the ground work that allows us to find those useful answers.

The Tarot cards stimulate ideas. And when we see those ideas we look at the cards with amazement instead of looking at the procedure they are used with. This has been the biggest misdirection of the Tarot cards. We keep looking at those cards instead of looking at the way our mind can tap into new levels of understanding.

Does the symbolism of Tarot cards have value?

The symbolism in the Tarot can help spark insight. But I do feel we have looked into that factor way too deeply trying to understand why the Tarot works. Studying every little aspect in each card has misled us from the real reason the Tarot has value.

We take every inch of Tarot procedures and card symbolism way too seriously. Too literally. Like driving to a destination and we see a sign marked on the road with an arrow that reads *"Destination Straight Ahead."* So we get out of our car and start climbing up the sign itself. This type of thinking leads us on a path to nowhere.

Is it really important that the Empress card in the Rider-Waite deck wears a crown of twelve stars signifying the zodiac? Or that the Fool in that same deck wears a red feather in his hat to represent passion? Is the image of Saturn branded on the Devil's right hand really that important to us? If it was, wouldn't all the Tarot decks made have those same details in them? The Thoth deck? The Tarot of Marseilles? So looking at the small details of the Tarot is just distracting us from what is really important in a reading. The application of how they are used to find constructive answers to questions asked.

How Tarot cards are used can now be seen as a very common and effective creative thinking technique known today as Conceptual Blending. This is something the mind naturally does. But only if we allow it to.

If you meet anyone who ever took a cognitive science course that covers Conceptual Blending and creative thinking techniques and you explain to them how a Tarot card reading is done, they will probably tell you that they have been taught the same identical applications and procedures.

I just looked online and found a course offered at Harvard University. The course is titled Creative Thinking: Innovative Solutions to Complex Challenges. The program is a two day course and it's full so there is a waiting list to get into it. This two day course cost $2,700. Now that's creative!

Renowned Tarotist and Mystic Paul Foster Case said, *"The most important use of the Tarot is to evoke thought."* I couldn't agree with him more. But during his time the capability of the Tarot was looked at as Esoteric study and Occult secrets. Not the understanding of the mind.

Now we know more about the mind then we did back then. Once you understand why card readings work it opens up the Tarot's potential into new mysteries never imagined. Not even by the master occultists or mystics from centuries past. The secrets of the Tarot are not lost in antiquity. They are found in it's future.

A Tarot card reading can now be seen as a creative thinking technique. Creative thinking techniques are commonly used to achieve objectives for the future. To see an outcome.

If you were to explain how to do a card reading to anyone who ever took creative thinking courses in college they would see the correlation right away.

Mapping the question out into sections called a card spread, adding a random stimulus called Tarot cards and conceptually blending the two are how all card readings are done. A very basic and effective creative thinking technique based on the way genius minds over the centuries have found answers to future objectives. In other words...to predict the future.

Understanding why Tarot cards work will help us advance forward with more effective applications than what's been done in the past.

mmmmm.... I see another chapter
in your future

2. Conceptual Blending & Tarot Cards

What is Conceptual Blending?

CONCEPTUAL BLENDING Defined:
 Conceptual blending refers to a set of cognitive operations for combining (or **blending**) words, images, and ideas in a network of "mental spaces" to create **meaning**. Also known as **conceptual** integration theory.

The best way to shake up an old pattern of thinking is to throw in a new, seemingly unrelated element. The mind will work overtime trying to fit it into that pattern — until it alters that pattern.

You take two remotely different things and force a connection between them. When your imagination finds a way to fill in the gaps – to connect the dots – to blend — that's when you come up with an unpredictable new idea.

Creativity is about combining and recombining different ideas. Today, cognitive science identifies this mode of thinking as Conceptual Blending.

Creativity in all domains, including science, technology, medicine, the arts, and day-to-day living, emerges from the basic mental operation of conceptually blending dissimilar subjects.

Combining the connection rich and metaphorical Tarot cards to elements of a question known as card spread positions uses this same procedure and for the same reasons. To find answers we didn't see before.

It's the kind of idea generator that provides a whole new level of insight. A radically altered way of thinking about a subject, category or question.

Conceptual Blending is combining two dissimilar concepts and using creative thinking to find similarities for answers to questions not previously seen. These associations are usually best done when they are viewed in a metaphoric sense of meaning.

Tarot cards are almost always associated to our questions from a metaphoric standpoint.

The psychological study and theory of Conceptual Blending was developed by Gilles Fauconnier and Mark Turner in 1993. It is a general theory of cognitive science to explain how our mind discovers new ideas and solves problems. It is our mind's natural method of finding new and original ideas and solutions.
It is a natural thinking technique that combines and recombines different ideas together.

Conceptual Blending is an emerging study for computer scientists wishing to pursue research into artificial intelligence. Tarot cards have been used as a centuries old form of artificial intelligence.

NOTE:
I think it's important to mention that Tarot cards and card spread positions are two separate parts of the card reading process. A position in a card spread is not just a place to lay a Tarot card. It is an aspect of a question being looked into. The Tarot cards placed into those positions are meant to spark ideas for answers to those particular sections of the question they are placed with.

I mention this because some sources on the subject imply that the card positions and the Tarot cards placed into those positions are one and the same. But they are as different from each other as a question is different from an answer.

How does this apply to Tarot cards?

It is a universal tendency to fragment a question into separate parts. This is what a card spread is made of – separate parts. Each position in a card spread is an aspect of a question being looked into. A Tarot card is placed into each position of the card spread and conceptually blended with the position's meaning to force our mind to see something new. A new idea. It is a technique to discover answers not seen before.

The Tarot cards have been a great source of 78 dissimilar subjects to be combined and recombined to elements of a question called card spread positions. Over the centuries this application has been recognized as fortune telling or divination. But today the Tarot card reading can be seen as using this very effective creative thinking technique. A way of thought that cognitive science has recognized and accepts as a substantial way of thinking creatively.

This explains the Tarot's success over the centuries to accurately make predictions to future objectives and problem solve. It has little to do with the cards themselves. It's the way the cards are applied to the question that makes them so successful.

The best way to stir up new ideas is to throw in a new, seemingly unrelated element, like a Tarot card into an aspect of your question. The mind will naturally work overtime trying to fit it into that aspect of the question until it finds something that makes sense. This allows our mind to see new ideas not normally seen with conventional thinking.

Its application is done by taking two remotely different things and forcing a connection between them. This is what we do when we associate a Tarot card to an element of a question known as a position in a card spread.

The Tarot cards, with their dreamlike images and vague meanings are perfect for making metaphorical associations for this type of thinking technique.

Metaphorical association is very common with this type of thought process. Metaphors allow us to make associations easily between one thing and another. Tarot cards are usually interpreted metaphorically for meaning to fit into a question being looked into.

A Tarot card reading triggers suggestions and ideas that pertain to a question being looked into. Sometimes these suggestions and ideas can lead to surprisingly original answers and solutions.

Any creative consultant today would see the similarities between creative thinking and a Tarot card reading right away as being identical applications of thought.

The purpose of this way of thought is always for the same reason. To make a prediction for a future objective whether by a creative consultant or a Tarot card reader. Both make predictions for a future objective being looked into. In other words predict the future.

Hey – I can get Google on here!

3. The Importance of Randomness

"A random stimulus is any class of creativity techniques that explores randomization. Most of their names start with the word "random," such as random word, random heuristic, random picture and random sound. In each random creativity technique, the user is presented with a random stimulus and explores associations that could trigger novel ideas. The power of random stimulus is that it can lead you to explore useful associations that would not emerge intentionally."
~Wikipedia

Adding a random element of any type to your question will lead to ideas that were not previously seen. Sometimes these ideas will lead to dynamic answers. Random elements added to sections of a question is a gateway application to find innovative answers that we can't think of with conventional thinking. Adding randomness to our questions sparks ideas.

What's important with randomness is you cannot steer the generated selection in any way. It must be selected randomly or the technique will lose its power to generate a new answer for you. It is one of the most basic and effective creative thinking techniques we know of today.

Anything around us can be used as a useful random stimulus. Nothing would be unacceptable no matter how unrelated the random subject is.

34   Radical Tarot – Breaking all the Rules

Here is a list of the 78 Tarot cards that can be randomly selected and associated with elements of a question being looked into. Any and all of these cards can be useful in finding answers to any aspect of any question looked into. It's up to your imagination to make useful connections.

•The Fool •The Magician •High Priestess •The Empress •The Emperor

•The Hierophant •The Lovers •The Chariot •Strength •The Hermit

•The Wheel of Fortune •Justice •The Hanged Man •Death • Temperance

•The Devil •The Tower •The Star •The Moon •The Sun • Judgment

•The World •Ace of Pentacles •Two Pentacles •Three Pentacles

•Four Pentacles •Five Pentacles •Six Pentacles •Seven Pentacles

•Eight Pentacles •Nine Pentacles •Ten Pentacles • Page of Pentacles

•Knight of Pentacles •Queen of Pentacles •King of Pentacles

•Ace of Wands •Two Wands •Three Wands • Four Wands •Five Wands

•Six Wands •Seven Wands •Eight Wands •Nine Wands • Ten Wands

•Page Wands •Knight Wands • Queen Wands •King Wands

•Ace of Swords •Two Swords •Three Swords •Four Swords •Five Swords

•Six Swords •Seven Swords • Eight Swords •Nine Swords •Ten Swords

• Page of Swords •Knight of Swords •Queen of Swords • King of Swords

•Ace of Cups •Two Cups •Three Cups •Four Cups •Five Cups • Six Cups

•Seven of Cups •Eight of Cups •Nine of Cups •Ten of Cups

•Page of Cups •Knight of Cups •Queen of Cups •King of Cups

The Importance of Randomness   35

Here is a list of 78 words that could be randomly selected and associated with elements of any question being looked into – just like Tarot cards are used. Anything in our world can be seen as a random stimulus. These are words we are all familiar with in our everyday world with no need to study and memorize.

bench envelope broom radio toast soap cup

umbrella book door window violin paint rose

bird sword insect light stamp gutter motor

ice dust fog rope mattress glue clock cash

car road zoo menu mouse aisle milk knot

seed pocket pipe ticket hammer circle needle

sky ocean octopus magnet Jell-O pot ring

notebook dictionary lobby library chimney

coffee ribcage mirrors flag helmet eye

cactus butterfly X-ray magazine screwdriver

ink ditches razor eyedropper artist storm fox

balloon sauce gum highway

These are just random things that we come across all the time. If we choose to make an association to a randomness, our mind will force itself to make connections in some way that makes sense

This is how ideas not previously seen are found as possible answers to questions. Randomly select one of these words above and interpret the word into elements of your question in ways that might be useful. Both of these list's are perfect tools for Conceptual blending.

Either one of these two lists would help you find answers to questions not seen before.

The Three Steps to creative thinking techniques:

Step #1 Choose a random word from the previous list.

Step #2 Jot down associations to an element of your question.

Step #3 Generate ideas. (Conceptual blending)

The Three Steps to using Tarot cards:

Step #1 Choose a random Tarot card.

Step #2 Interpret associations to a position of your card spread.

Step #3 Generate ideas. (Reading Tarot cards)

Defining things too closely:

Although definitions are useful, they can create meanings that work like blinders. Limiting our perception of meaning. I feel that the way we go about defining the Tarot cards limits range. This can lead us to use paint-by-numbers interpretations of the cards.

We are all familiar with the subjects in the 78 word list and we would not need to study them in depth for meaning. We could also find useful meanings to questions with that list if we chose to. We would not need to study the meanings or ponder their symbolism. We wouldn't need to memorize sentenced definitions to each word's "correct" meaning to use them for ideas to questions.

Do we define Tarot cards too closely? Here are three items from that word list defined in ways I feel we define Tarot cards. Notice how defining narrows their meaning. You can see much more in these items than is defined here. Does defining the Tarot limit range of meaning as well?

Definitions for: BENCH....KNOT.....MAGAZINE

BENCH DEFINITION:
The bench represents a resting place. It stands for a sturdy sanctuary. A time to rest. Things seem to be at a time to sit and think. A time for inaction. Staying put. Stable. Resting place.

BENCH REVERSED:
A time for action and not to sit down. Things are not as they should be at this time for sitting still. A need to move on.

KNOT DEFINITION:
The knot is seen as a strong bond. A unity. Interaction is seen in the knot. Working together to create a union. Tying things together.

KNOT REVERSED: Tangled. Snags in the situation. Confusing mess. Beware of actions that are hard to undo.

MAGAZINE MEANING:
The magazine represents many aspects to see. Information is near. Hidden knowledge until the page is turned. A time to learn more about what you are seeking. Information at your fingertips.

MAGAZINE REVERSED:
Magazine reversed means messages hard to read. A need to put things in the right direction to proceed. Confusion and things not seen in the right way. Misunderstood messages. Things make no sense until polarity is aligned. North and south transfixed!

Definitions are useful and even necessary but they can limit our range of perception. Do we do this with Tarot card meanings?

The definitions above are short and limited to make a point. But a professional reading could very well be accomplished by using the word list as easily as by using the Tarot card list. The ideas that can arise would be endless with either source.

We could spend years of deep study with that list of 78 words. We could become authorities on that list of 78 words. But would it really help us?

Randomness can come from anywhere in our world. And when we connect the randomness into segments of our question we force ourselves to see things we didn't see before.

EXAMPLES OF INVENTIONS MADE FROM CONCEPTUALLY BLENDING RANDOMNESS:

The Hubble telescope — a shower head
The pendulum clock — a swinging thurible
Gutenberg's printing press — a wine press
Pop-open canned goods —the pea pod
Braille for the blind — the pine cone
The heat seeking missile — the Sidewinder rattlesnake
Newtons theory of gravity — a fallen apple?
How sound travels – DaVinci seeing ripples in a pond of water
Velcro — seed-bearing burrs from plants

Random stimulus can come from anywhere if we have the imagination to see it.

The 78 Tarot cards are a perfect set of random ideas. They are connection rich and can show us many angles to a question. The Tarot cards meanings can go on infinitely. Which is what makes them so rich for this type of thinking. But we are not limited to only using those cards for a source of randomness to spark new ideas.

Everything we create has been done by combining something we are already familiar with to a question we seek to understand more about.

Hubble Telescope:
The focus of the Hubble telescope was figured out by looking at a shower head adjusting the flow of water.

The pendulum clock:
The theory for the pendulum clock was seen by Galileo while sitting in church watching a priest swing an incense filled thurible during mass.

The printing press:
Gutenberg was watching someone work a wine press and thought of how he could use that concept to press ink onto paper. His first printing press was a makeshift wine press.

The pop open can:
The idea of can goods with pop open tops came from an inventor looking at a pea pod from his garden. The pea pod has a natural weak seam along the edge making it easier to open the pod along that seam.

Braille:
A blind man contemplated patterns that could be recognized to create words through touch by holding a pine cone in his hand.

The Heat Seeking Missile:
The heat seeking missile was thought of by thinking of the way the Sidewinder rattlesnake attacks its prey. It senses its victim's body heat. The first heat seeking missile was named the *Sidewinder* for that reason.

Your imagination will branch out into endless thoughts if you just allow it to. And imagination is the gateway to your intuition.

Do not read this chapter without wearing your magical hoodie robe.

4. Finding Meaning in the Cards

"The Tarot shows an endless source of meanings, all coming from one source....You."
~ Vincent Pitisci

If there is one thing the Tarot offers it is a wide variety of meanings to the cards. Some sources meanings are different than others. This can make learning the cards challenging at best. Which source is the best to follow? They all seem to make sense.
And they all seem to work.

Keyword Meanings –

After years of study I have found that keyword meanings encompass the most value to the Tarot. Keywords offer a larger range of meaning than sentences can give us. Sentences imply a card has specific meaning. The more you define something, the more limited it becomes. The more specific the meaning is – the less it is capable of meaning something else. Specific meanings reduce the range of possibilities the cards can show us.

Limitations shorten the range that can be seen in the cards. Seeing we have no known source of origin or purpose to the Tarot, we really have no "correct" or original meaning assigned to each card. This is why you will see card meanings vary from one source to another depending on the author's way of seeing each card.

Keyword meanings allow us to receive an endless array of meaning in a Tarot card. This allows us to fit the card to an element of a question easier than using detailed and specific Tarot card definitions.

Reverse Meanings –

If you exclude reverse meanings, it still would be physically impossible to go through all of the various combinations of meanings the 78 Tarot cards can show you. One lifetime would not be a sufficient amount of time to cover them all.

I do not use reverse meanings. I know many wonderful readers that use them and if you choose to, I'm sure it will work out fine. Although I teach and write using the Rider Waite deck, I use the Tarot of Marseilles deck when I read for clients. Reverse meanings were not used at all in the printed material I learned with back when I first started reading. If a card is laid up side down I simply turn it right side up. All cards face me the reader, and I read them the way they were created, right side up, not upside down.

If you feel you might like to use reverse meanings and you're just starting out, I would suggest first learning the Tarot without them. Then, if you feel you still need more insight into your readings, add reverse meanings to your method of using the Tarot. I feel you will find much insight without them. At least I did. More than you need! But reverse meanings will give you another aspect of the cards to look at.

The combinations of cards being laid into a card spread without reverse meanings are in the many billions.

Reading the cards is like dancing. Everyone moves their own way to the music. You will find what works best for you as you move forward with the Tarot. In the meantime you are more than welcome to use any or all of my methods as much as you like.

I have added a Quick Reference Guide in this chapter for easy card meaning reference as you read on.

The Minor Arcana

Quick Reference List: The 56 Minor Arcana

Card	Meaning
Aces	New Concept
Twos	Choice
Threes	Creativity
Fours	Stability
Fives	Change
Sixes	Perseverance
Sevens	Confidence
Eights	Advancement
Nines	Accomplishment
Tens	Completion
Pages	New Paths
Knights	Action
Queens	Patience and Understanding
Kings	Knowledge

The Four Suits

Suit	Definitions
Swords/ Spades	Thought
Pentacles/Diamonds	The Physical/Material
Wands/Clubs	The Spirit
Cups/Hearts	Emotion

Note: I have used a common definition for all four cards of each suit. The suit definition will show you how the card is defined specifically. Example: Aces are defined as "New Concept". Therefore the Ace of Swords would be a new concept in your thinking. The Ace of Cups would be a new sense in your emotions. The Five of Wands would be "Change in your Spirit." And so on.

The Minor Arcana

The experience of life is remarkable and it consists of a collection of stages that can be seen in the pips of the Minor Arcana. Whether these issues are big or small makes no difference. They are mirrored in the cards as the stages we go through with everything we do.

The Tarot cards Minor Arcana breaks these issues into ten stages. Ace through ten. Each stage is necessary to go through before moving on to the next stage. They show a pattern that we all go through on various issues and pursuits in our lives. That's life.

Understanding patterns help us to make predictions.
With this seen, we now can see what stage our client is currently in as they sit with you. This means we also know what stages they have already gone through (past) and what stages they will be heading for (future).

Most people coming to you for a reading will be in the middle of the "Fives" on their quest. This is why they seek you out for answers. "Change." Many changes are disruptive which is why the images on the "Fives" all seem so negative. Some clients are bored to death being stuck in the stable "Fours" as well. I don't think I have ever had anyone in all my years sit across from me while they are in the happy attainment of the "Nines".

The Court Cards:

The court cards are specific actions or ways of thinking. At one time the court cards were seen as people. That was before there were pictures of people doing things on all the cards. Now any of the cards can be seen as representing people as there are people in most of the whole Tarot deck. If you choose to use a significator (a card to represent the client) then the court cards work well for this. Otherwise they offer meaning just like the rest of the deck.

Significator cards are used as follows:
Kings represent men – Queens represent women – Knights represent boys and Pages represent girls. You would decide which one to choose for your client as a significator. I personally do not use a significator in my readings. So the court cards are just read like the rest of the Minor Arcana.

The 10 stages of the Minor Arcana's Ace thru 10

Everything starts with an idea. This holds true whether we are contemplating something big like marriage or small everyday affairs.

First the idea has to come into our mind. The Aces represent the *Idea*.

The Twos represent the *Choice* we make, yes or no, on moving forward with that idea.

If we decide to move forward with the idea we *Create* it with the Threes.

Once we create the idea we *Stabilize* it, seen in the Fours.

Then, if anything changes at all, it becomes a disruption.
The Fives are disruption. *Change*.

The Sixes show us overcoming the obstacles of the changes of the Fives as we *Persevere*.

And once we overcome the obstacles as seen in the Sixes, we become more *Confident* in ourselves, seen in the Sevens.

With that confidence we *Advance* in our quest, seen with the Eights.

As we advance we *Attain* what we sought to have with the Nines. The Nines show us achieving our quest.

Which leads us to the Tens. Ultimately we see it through to its totality. To a *Completion* in the Tens.

All things must come to an end someday but we can look back and say we followed it through to the end and a successful and rewarding experience.

The Tens are an end of a cycle. The end of one cycle means the start of another cycle. Like layers. So a quest can have many layers of cycles as we experience it. Many disruptions and many accomplishments is what our life journey is all about.

The Court Cards

The court cards break away from the pips with their own specific attributes.

Their meanings are not part of the sequence of the pips. They represent other aspects that can be useful in the reading. A new direction, taking actions, having patience and knowledge itself.

The court cards have been seen in many ways. They have even been used to describe physical attributes of a person. The tall dark handsome stranger you are going to meet was the King of Wands. The King of Swords was seen as a professional with fair complexion and blond hair. The Queen of Swords was a mean but beautiful woman and the Queen of Cups was the loving fair maiden. I don't feel this type of thing helps much in today's readings. More focus on the essence of the card's meaning seems to give better results.

Kings represent knowledge. Whether it means you have knowledge as an asset or you need to attain that knowledge would depend on the reading itself.

Queens represent patience. Patience is easier if you have a good understanding on the situation. So understanding the situation helps a person to keep patient with things. Or maybe you have too much patience and that is creating an obstacle for you. The reader would decide.

Knights represent action. Whether action being taken is not a wise choice or action that needs to be taken is vital at this point depends on the reading. The reader will decide.

Pages represent a new beginning. New direction that might need to be taken or maybe a new direction that the seeker is on right now. Either way Pages represent a new path.

The gender has no bearing on these cards and all the cards can be seen as aspects for either sex. A King's knowledge for a woman or the Queen's patience and understanding for a man.

Understanding the Four Suits:

Think of the suits like a spice added to the stew. They can give flavor to meaning but they are not the main component. They accent the card's meaning. I feel focusing on the numeric value of the Minor Arcana is most important. The suit gives accent to the numeric value if it is used at all.

The four suits represent the four basic functions of our consciousness. They are: Swords –Thought / Cups – Emotions / Wands – Spirit / Pentacles – Material world.

Suits Description:

ACES: New Concept
Swords: New concept regarding my thinking
Cups: New concept regarding my feelings
Wands: New concept regarding my spirit
Pentacles: New concept about my physical world
— But an overall new concept regardless of the suit.

TWOS: Choice
Swords: A choice based on my reasoning
Cups: A choice based on my feelings
Wands: A choice based on my true spirit
Pentacles: A choice based on my material world
— An overall feeling of making a choice regardless of the suit.

THREES: Creativity
Swords: Creation from my thoughts
Cups: Creation based on my feelings
Wands: Creation stemming from my spirit
Pentacles: Creation from my physical environment
— Overall creating from my essence.

FOURS: Stability
Swords: Stability in my thinking
Cups: Stability in my feelings
Wands: Stability in my soul
Pentacles: Stability in my material world
— Overall stability in my situation.

FIVES: Change
Swords: Changes in my thinking
Cups: Changes in my feelings
Wands: Change in my spirit
Pentacles: Change in my material world
— Overall change in my life.

SIXES: Perseverance
Swords: Perseverance with my idea
Cups: Perseverance with my way of feeling
Wands: Perseverance within my soul
Pentacles: Perseverance in my material goals
—Overall perseverance in who I am and what I'm doing.

SEVENS: Confidence
Swords: Confidence in my ideas
Cups: Confidence in my feelings
Wands: Confidence in my spirit
Pentacles: Confidence in my physical abilities
—Overall confidence in myself.

EIGHTS: Advancement
Swords: Advancement in my thinking
Cups: Advancement in allowing my feelings to come out
Wands: Advancement in my spirit
Pentacles: Advancement in my material world
— Overall advancement in my life's progress.

NINES: Attainment
Swords: Attainment of awareness
Cups: Attainment of true feelings
Wands: Attainment of my soul's quest
Pentacles: Attainment of my material desires
— Overall attainment of my pursuits of happiness.

TENS: Completion
Swords: Completion accomplished in my thoughts
Cups: Completion accomplished with my feelings
Wands: Completion accomplished from my soul
Pentacles: Completion accomplished in a material sense
— Overall completion of a quest.

PAGES: New Path
Swords: A new path in my thinking
Cups: A new path concerning my feelings
Wands: A new path in regards to my spirit
Pentacles: A new path on my physical wants
— Overall new path or direction.

KNIGHTS: Action
Swords: Action taken based on my thinking
Cups: Action taken based on my feelings
Wands: Action taken based on my spirit
Pentacles: Action taken based on my physical necessities
— Overall action needs to be taken.

QUEENS: Patience
Swords: Patience with my thoughts
Cups: Patience with my feelings
Wands: Patience with my spirit
Pentacles: Patience with my physical world
— Overall a time for, or a presence of patience.

KINGS: Knowledge
Swords: New knowledge in my thinking
Cups: New knowledge about my true feelings
Wands: New knowledge from my very soul
Pentacles: New knowledge about my physical world
— Overall new knowledge is needed or is gained.

This gives you a general insight as to the suits and how they can work with the meaning of the cards.
Most concerns a client has will affect all four aspects of their consciousness to some degree.

The Aces
Possible Meaning
~ New Concepts ~

 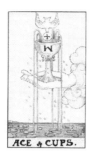  

New ideas and direction into a new endeavor.

The Aces represent a new look. A fresh start or new concept. New opportunity is around us all the time but becoming aware of it is what is key here.

An epiphany is seen in the Swords. A new love in the Cups. A new inspiration in the Wands and a new home or career in the Pentacles. But there are many other new things that can be associated to these four cards.

Anything from new challenges to something like a child for a young couple.

A change of heart. A change in plans.
A new strategy to an old idea.

The Idea

Boundless · Opportunity · Discovery · Promising · A Source

Aces
New Concept

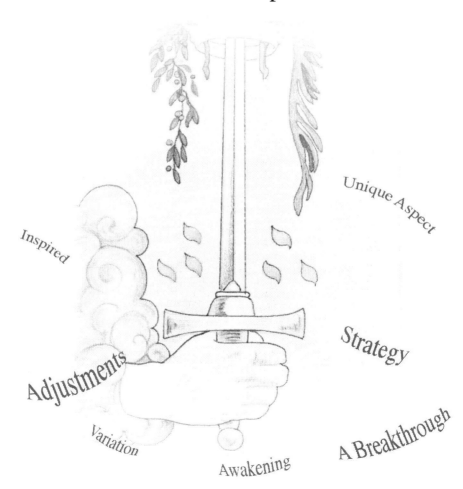

Inspired · Unique Aspect · Adjustments · Strategy · Variation · Awakening · A Breakthrough

The Twos
Possible Meaning
~ Choice ~

If the new idea is taken from the Aces, we proceed and move forward. The choice is made. The twos represent choice. Choosing yes or no on a specific concept. Once the choice is made, we can decide on continuing on our life's journey. But the choice has to be made in order for that to happen. Which path do we take. Right or left. East or west. The Twos represent that time in our question. A time to decide. Sometimes this choice can be difficult.

Sometimes we need to gather more information before we can proceed as seen in the blindfolded Two of Swords. Or a need to juggle the idea around awhile as seen in the Two of Pentacles. Weighing out the big picture before we decide as seen in the Two of Wands and exploring the possibilities of a deep bond as seen in the Two of Cups.

Whatever it is, we can see that the twos spark an idea to choose. A choice is key at this time and should be looked into deeper.

Making the Choice

Balanced Unsure Needed Decision
Undecided Sincere Offer

Twos
Choice

Two Minds Possibilities
Chosen Path Duality Torn Between
Proposition Speculation

The Threes
Possible Meaning
~ Creativity ~

If the decision in the Twos was to move forward on our decision then the next step is to create the situation. The Threes represent building the situation.

Laying down the initial groundwork. The whole beginning of actually creating the situation. In the Three of Pentacles we see someone who's building a church and is recognized as capable in his work.

The Three of Cups shows a celebration of a newly created relationship. Maybe an engagement between two people.

The Three of Swords shows facing an awareness of a sad truth that is now being painfully addressed.

And the Three of Wands shows a look at all of the new horizons we have to work with.

The Threes are an exciting phase in our journey through our objective as we move down this path. It shows all sorts of newness and possibilities to work with. Creating a freshness of something new and ultimately growing our life experience.

Finding Meaning in the Cards   55

Creating the Situation

Preliminaries Restoring Blossoming Celebration New Feelings

Threes
Creativity

Building Flourishing Planning Inspiring Exploration Curiosity Recuperation

The Fours
Possible Meaning
~ Stability ~

Once the creative energy of the Threes has been established we move to the Stability of the Fours. This step is now to settle in to a routine and a predictable and secure situation. Something we can count on to be there.

The Four of Pentacles now has his wealth from building his church in the Three of Pentacles and that wealth seems very important to him.

The Four of Cups seems sort of melancholy about the routine set up in the new relationship. Almost as if bored with the daily routine.

The Four of Swords can be seen as an end to the sad truth that was faced in the Three of Swords.

The Four of Wands seems to show a welcoming home to someone. And home is the most stable thing we all can relate to.

Whatever the question happens to be, the Fours seem to show us stability in some way.

Finding Meaning in the Cards

Stabilizing the Situation

Predictable Familiarity Organized
Structured Calculated

Fours
Stability

Anchored Grounded
Established Safe Routine
Calming Methodical

The Fives
Possible Meaning
~ Change ~

If anything changes from stability it would seem disruptive. No one likes change once things are regulated and routines have been established.

Here we can see the architect from the Three of Pentacles walking past the very church he created. Only now things seem to have taken a turn for the worse for him and his wife. Disruption from the safe Fours has taken place.

The stable and routine relationship in the Four of Cups seems to have taken a sad loss as three of the cups have spilled unto the ground. Sadness, remorse or regret are seen.

A recent change or disruption has taken place in the Five of Swords as two men walk away from a disruptive scene.

And the peaceful Four of Wands has turned into a quarrel that seems chaotic and confusing in the Five of Wands.

The fives show change and change can be good or it can be bad. But usually it is not something we enjoy experiencing. Even if it's something we know needs to happen. But changes can also strengthen and temper a situation as will be shown in the next cards. The Sixes.

Finding Meaning in the Cards 59

Challenges to the Situation

Tension
Undoing
Stimulation
Shifting
Challenging

Fives
Change

Conflict
Adjustments
Disruption
Scattered Energy
Delay
Opposition
Differences

The Sixes
Possible Meaning
~ Perseverance ~

The Sixes show us that if we continue, we will persevere. We eventually overcome our challenges and break down obstacles that seem to get in the way. We learn to move on and try again but only now with more experience. More knowledge. Wiser than before.

Here we see the architect who built the church in the Three of Pentacles giving money to the poor. He has been in their position and understands true value more than before when we saw him in the Four of Pentacles clinging onto his precious coins.

The Six of Cups shows two coming together with a new fresh start, like children starting off new.

The Six of Swords shows moving on to a calmer shore to heal from the past.

The Six of Wands shows someone coming home as the victor from the quarrelsome Five of Wands.

The Sixes show us overcoming our challenges.

Finding Meaning in the Cards 61

Overcoming the Challenge

Optimism   Resolution   Foresight
Diplomacy   Leadership

Sixes
Perseverance

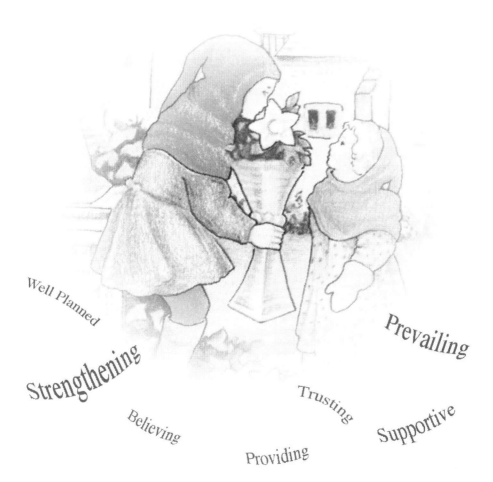

Well Planned   Prevailing
Strengthening   Trusting   Supportive
Believing   Providing

The Sevens
Possible Meaning
~ Confidence ~

The Sevens allow us to take a look at what we've accomplished. To see our achievements. To see in ourselves the confidence that we can accomplish in our quest.

Looking at our progress is seen clearly in the Seven of Pentacles.

The Seven of Cups shows all the accomplishments that have been made gleaming in front of you.

The Seven of Swords shows a confident thief who knows his prowess can give him an edge in the coming battle.

The Seven of Wands bravely holds off opposition that is threatening as he confidently stands his ground.

The Sevens are a time in our journey where we find our true worth. We come to realize our strengths and we come to realize we are able to achieve the things we want to.

Finding Meaning in the Cards 63

Confidence in the situation

Prepared Skillful Cunning
Convincing Resourceful

Sevens
Confidence

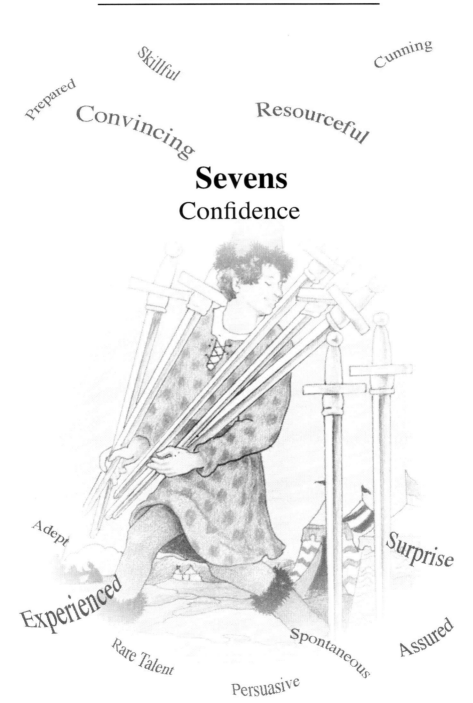

Adept Surprise
Experienced Spontaneous Assured
Rare Talent Persuasive

The Eights
Possible Meaning
~ Advancement ~

After confidence is gained with the Sevens we move forward and advance on our goal with the Eights.

We start to see real progress in the Eight of Pentacles.

The Eight of Cups shows many cups accumulated as we search for even more.

The Eight of Swords shows a need to free ourselves of self-imposed restrictions and take off the blindfold to advance forward.

And the Eight of Wands shows clear sailing with no restrictions in our way as Wands sail easily through the air.

The Eights are showing a time in our quest of seeing real progress.
Or in the case of the Swords we see a need to take away restrictions so we can advance forward. But the topic is advancement.

I don't agree with Waite's illustration of the Eight of Swords. Showing a lack of advancement instead of advancement. Waite decided to show a negative tone to the suit of Swords, especially in the Eight, Nine and Ten of Swords. These cards seem to depict the essence they represent in a negative manner. Or a lack of the essence they represent.

Moving forward in the situation

Progress *Positive Action* *Precise*
No Resistance *Concentration*

Eights
Advancement

Made Clear *Expansion*
Visionary *Alignment* *A Breakthrough*
Quality *On Course*

The Nines
Possible Meaning
~ Attainment ~

Once we start moving forward and advancing with the Eights we open up opportunity and attain our final objective. To reach what we've been searching to attain all along.

We can see attainment of our goal in the Nine of Pentacles as a lush estate and a peaceful home.

The Nine of Cups shows a happy person with his many cups as he sits comfortably with a smiling face.

The Nine of Swords shows an attainment of a sad truth. A realization and coming to terms with what must be faced to attain what we need.

And the Nine of Wands shows someone who has struggled and fought to attain what he wanted. But the struggle was worth it and now it is his to keep.

The Nines are the cards of Attainment. It took many steps to get here but our efforts have paid off in the end.

Finding Meaning in the Cards 67

Attaining the Situation

Freedom
Acquired *Secure* *Valuable*
Aspiration

Nines
Attainment

Growth *Realization*
Successful *Epiphany* *Well Positioned*
Generosity *Availability*

The Tens
Possible Meaning
~ Completion ~

Once we've attained our quest in the Nines there is a time that comes as an end.

A time to gather all our accomplishments and move on is seen in the Ten of Wands.

A man sits peacefully in his beautiful home enjoying the family he raised in the Ten of Pentacles.

The Ten of Cups shows a family looking at all they have accomplished together.

And the Ten of Swords shows a completion to a sad truth that needed to be addressed. Tens are a completion. All things end and we can look back and say, "Well done."

What a wonderful journey. The Ace through Ten is the cycle we go through on major quests in our life as well as minor accomplishments. Some layers are major and some seem minor. Accomplishing a wonderful marriage and raising a family with the Ten of Cups, or quitting smoking seen as the end of the cigarette smoker in the Ten of Swords and the start of a healthier life style.

Finding Meaning in the Cards 69

Completion of a Quest

Wholeness
Journey's End
Peace
Closure
Totality

Tens
Completion

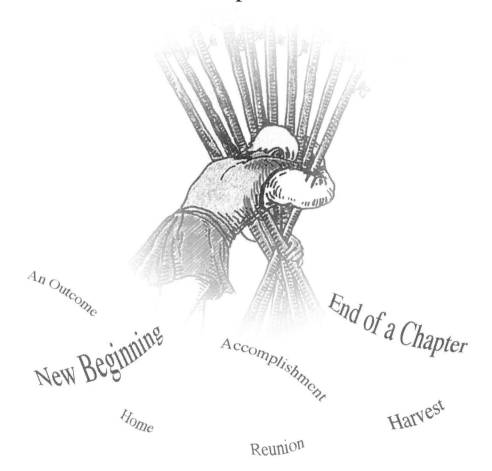

An Outcome
End of a Chapter
New Beginning
Accomplishment
Harvest
Home
Reunion

The 4 Pages
Possible Meaning
~ New Paths ~

The Pages represent new paths. A new direction or plan. A new opportunity is seen.

A new direction in my thinking is seen in the Page of Swords.

A new direction in my feelings is seen in the Page of Cups.

A new inspiration is seen in the Page of Wands.

A new direction in your material world in the Page of Pentacles. A new career, a new home, raise in income. It could mean finding a new interest.

Any new direction can be seen in the Pages.

Finding Meaning in the Cards 71

A New Direction

Seeking Adventure The Unknown

Fresh Start New Reality

Pages
New Path

Acceptance Radical Shift

Chosen Path Untraveled Territory Imagination

Initiation

The 4 Knights
Possible Meaning
~ Taking Action ~

The four Knights represent action. Sometimes having patience is best and sometimes taking action is the answer.

When the Knights come up in a reading it sparks a look at a time to take action. Time to make a move. Change jobs. Re-evaluate a relationship.

Stir things up and rearrange the furniture. Sometimes we cannot take action. The Knights can show an opportunity for that to change in your favor.

Actions taken based on what I know – Swords

Action taken based on how I feel in my heart – Cups

Action taken based on my spirit – Wands

Action taken based on the physical situation – Pentacles

Taking Initiative

Charismatic
Diligence *Credibility* *Service*
Initiative

Knights
Action

A Challenge *Execution of Ideas* *Allegiance*
Effortless
Passion *Loyalty*
A Clear Objective

The 4 Queens
Possible Meaning
~ Having Patience ~

The Queens represent a time for patience and understanding. Grace and dignity in the actions you take.

Quiet knowledge. Knowledge known but not spoken. Hidden source and alliance. Attraction to your views.

The energy of alliances. A loyal partner. An influential source. Quiet perception is to your advantage. Observation without action.

The Queens represent a loyal ally. Someone who knows much about your objective.

Someone who shares your concerns.

Patience and understanding after thinking it through – Swords

Patience and understanding based on my true feelings – Cups

Patience and understanding from my spirit – Wands

Patience and understanding based on my physical world – Pentacles

Finding Meaning in the Cards 75

Having the Patience

Sensitivity Tenderness Graceful Influence

Understanding Dignity

Queens
Patience

High Ranking

Enduring Eloquence

Elegant Strength Perceptive Sternness

Insightful

The 4 Kings
Possible Meaning
~ Acquiring Knowledge ~

The Kings represent knowledge. Gathering information on an objective before action is taken. A need to gain more insight.
The Kings can also represent someone who has the knowledge you seek to know. An honest and loyal source. Someone who has the answers. A person who can help you to your goal.

An authority on the subject you are involved with. Knowledge in your quest. A master on the subject. An influential person.
A successful outcome. Recognized authority in your favor.

A need to master the quest you seek to take.

Careful thought will bring solutions – Swords

My feelings will bring the right decision – Cups

My spirit will guide my awareness on this issue – Wands

My material world holds the answers I seek – Pentacles

Having the Knowledge

Proficient Disciplined Authoritative
Unwavering Influencial

Kings
Knowledge

Commited

Licensed Innovator

Mature

Clearly Understood Analytical Straight Forward

The Major Arcana.

I do feel these 22 Major Arcana are all linked to each other. The Major Arcana are said to represent deep universal principles and metaphysical concepts. This type of thinking would be good for self study.
 In a card reading the Minor Arcana show patterns in our life's journey. The Major Arcana can accent the reading with insight into attributes the client should focus on.

They have no sequential pattern of thought but we can all relate to their energy. Songs are written expressing the essence of the Major Arcana. Love, Truth, Solitude, Harmony and so on. Our quest to understand what life is about or its purpose is what these cards try to represent.

The Major Arcana images can best be described as making sense but not making sense simultaneously. Their dreamlike images can spark great insight into the reading. They can help us on our path by showing us a scope of universal perceptions that help us understand aspects of our journey.

They have an endless scope of meaning to be associated to our quest. They can also be toned down to fit into our everyday concerns to show some type of meaning that might be beneficial to see. The dreamlike images of these cards can spark wonderful insight into our question.

You will find many sources of meaning on these 22 cards, with many different tilts, twist and turns. My thinking of the Majors meanings change as I continue on my journey. This is how I see the meanings today. They might be different than some other sources. That's OK.

The 22 Major Arcana

Quick Reference List: The 22 Major Arcana

Number	Card	Meaning
0	The Fool	Believing
1	The Magician	Awareness
2	The High Priestess	Mystery
3	The Empress	Creativity
4	The Emperor	Leadership
5	The Hierophant	Guidance
6	The Lovers	Duality
7	The Chariot	Ability
8	Strength	Fortitude
9	The Hermit	Seclusion
10	The Wheel	Destiny
11	Justice	Balance
12	The Hanged Man	Sacrifice
13	Death	Transition
14	Temperance	Inspiration
15	The Devil	False Fears
16	The Tower	Disruption
17	The Star	Direction
18	The Moon	Mysterious Paths
19	The Sun	Nurturing
20	Judgement	Awakening
21	The World	Perfect Balance

Note: Some Tarot decks have the *Strength VIII* and the *Justice XI* cards numerical values transposed. *Justice* still keeps its meaning of *Truth*, and *Strength* still keeps its meaning of *Mind & Body*.

The Fool 0

Possible Meaning
~ Believing ~

The Fool represents a carefree attitude. No restrictions or roots to follow.

Seeing the world as open for suggestions and come-what-may thinking.

No responsibilities, obligations or commitment.

This card can also show naivety, inexperience and innocence. Taking action before thinking things out fully. No caution or thought of consequence. Recklessly optimistic. But a happy spirit until something goes wrong. No clear focus or direction. A wanderer. Traveler with no specific home or destination. A footloose attitude. Carefree with minimal responsibilities or obligations.

Not a part of the establishment. In a vulnerable position. Not prepared. Living strictly in the moment with no thought of tomorrow.

Much to learn on a new concept or objective. New territory with much to explore and learn about.

A new quest with little experience to help you find direction. Much to learn as you move forward on a new endeavor.

Blind trust without any real plan to your objective.

Playful

Hopeful

Dreamer

Free Spirit

Blind Trust

Innocence

The Fool 0
Believing

Care Free

Free Thinker

Non-Conforming

Unpredictable

Wild Card

Impulsive

Uncaring

The Magician I

Possible Meaning
~ Awareness ~

The Magician's essence can signify calculated and careful planning. Seeing clearly what others cannot see.

Plans are thought out before action is taken. A need to focus on detail.

Confidence in the actions taken. Attracting total attention to your actions. Being able to surprise those around you with your actions.

Practiced and well done execution.
Knowing all the facts before moving forward. Understanding all angles of the situation. A person very capable to achieve an objective sought, once plans are in place.

Give your direction careful thought before proceeding. You could pull a rabbit out of a hat!

Putting yourself in a good position to convince others around you. You are capable of impressive action to convince others and sway opinions.

A need to do what most might feel is impossible but if carefully thought through you find a way to succeed.

A master in one's craft.

Finding Meaning in the Cards 83

Manifestation

Confidence Cunning Creative Genius Ingenuity
Mastership

The Magician I
Awareness

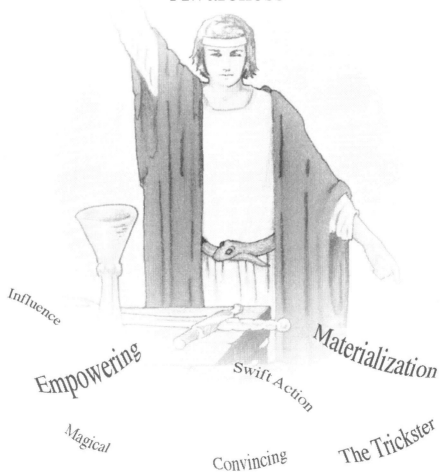

Influence Empowering Swift Action Materialization
Magical Convincing The Trickster

The High Priestess II

Possible Meaning

Mystery

Hidden knowledge and the unknown is seen in the High Priestess.

Information that still needs to be understood before proceeding. A need to see more than is currently at your disposal.

It is to your advantage to look deeper before progressing forward. More to be seen is still ahead.
Walking a fine line between logic and intuition while making a decision.

Hidden alliance.

Listen to your inner voice to see another option. A wise influence is near. Listen to your heart as well as your head. Answers are found within.

A dreamscape is experienced if the mind is allowed to drift. Guidance from an unexplainable source.

Secrets are revealed.

The mysterious and unattainable.

Dreams could show meaning at this time.

Finding Meaning in the Cards   85

Serenity

Intuition Silence Dreamscapes Secretive
Mystical

The High Priestess II
Mystery

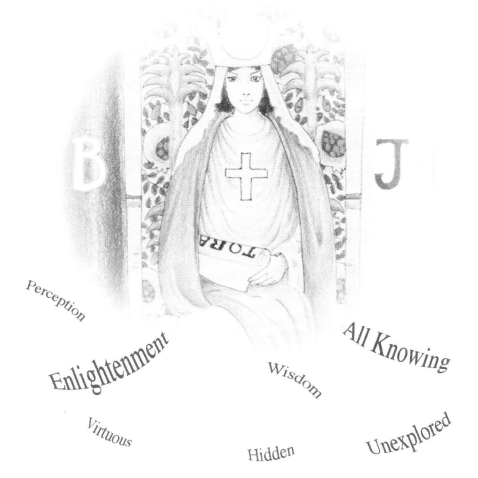

Perception Enlightenment Wisdom All Knowing
Virtuous Hidden Unexplored

The Empress III

Possible Meaning
~ Creativity ~

The Empress represents abundance and growth. She is the force of creativity. The mother and the nurturer.

This card can be seen as a time for new ideas to flourish.

A need to see new perceptions and innovative accomplishments. Life-giving energy. Plentiful environment.

A time for new directions and opportunity.

Something new is coming soon.

A new gateway or path is seen.

A need to focus on your creative inspiration. A time to let ideas flow into realities. The Empress can connect new dimensions of awareness. Prosperity and happiness. Care and true commitment to a cause. Unshakable dedication to a concept coming from the heart.

Successful outcomes can flourish if desired.

The Mother

Plentiful *Abundance* *Conceived*
Fertile *Bountiful*

The Empress III
Creativity

Generous *Nurturing* *Harvest* *Essence of Life*
Richness *Healing* *Manifestation*

The Emperor IV

Possible Meaning
~ Leadership ~

Accomplishment of an objective.

Taking action on an idea in effective ways.

The ideas have been agreed upon, now action is taken. Planned execution of an objective.

Leadership taken on a specific purpose.

Taking initiative in constructive ways that lead to successful outcomes.

The Emperor has the authority and the knowledge to create and execute objectives being sought.

A builder of material accomplishments. Advancement and progress.

The power of the Emperor is vision to see a goal's finished outcome before it is created.

This card can represent strong foundations to build upon. Established and influential sources. Material gain is seen in this card. Progress if efforts are taken.

Opportunities and need for leadership are both seen in this card.

Manifesting ideas into realities.

Finding Meaning in the Cards

Development

Motivator · The Builder · Authority · To Manifest · Initiative

The Emperor IV
Leadership

Reliance · Established · Planned Strategy · Successful Action · Visionary · Fairness · Strong Trust

The Hierophant V

Possible Meaning
~ Guidance ~

Playing by the rules. Aboveboard and sincere advice from a higher authority.

Influence from a higher source. Precise procedures are expected to be followed. Rules are enforced.

Tradition is a strong influence. Playing by the book.
Conforming to what has been done in the past.

Tried and true knowledge from past experiences are applied for successful outcomes.

Sincere efforts from a select source of influence. Good advice for all involved can be found.

Old ways are still set in place. Choosing constructive and proven positive options.

Time-tested methods are best option.
Obeying the rules for a positive end result.

Established set of rules and procedures are best to be followed at this time.

High counsel.

A celebrated source of guidance.

Higher Influence

Counsel · Atonement · Community
Compliance · Guardianship
Tradition

The Hierophant V
Guidance

Ritualistic · Ceremony · Dedication · Forgiving · Obedience · Conformity

The Lovers VI

Possible Meaning
~ Duality ~

An understanding of both sides.

Polarity is a strong influence. Differences good and bad come together. Seeing more than one side.

Understanding and loving viewpoints that are not your own. Sharing one's spirit with another close to the heart.

The quest for an interaction with another side of life. A union of inspiring ideas.

A coming together. Attraction to an opposite energy. Harmony in life with another. A choice between two forces.

Temptation can sway an important decision. A coming together of opposite choices.

Sparks that can start fires. Decisions made from the heart.

A time to consider committed partnerships.

Choices made from the heart. Sacrifices for another close by and on the same path.

An everlasting spiritual unity. A compromise of ideas in a partnership from the heart.

Seeing and understanding both sides of self.

The Mirrored Self

Polarity · Choice · Magnetism
Engaging · Involvement

The Lovers VI
Duality

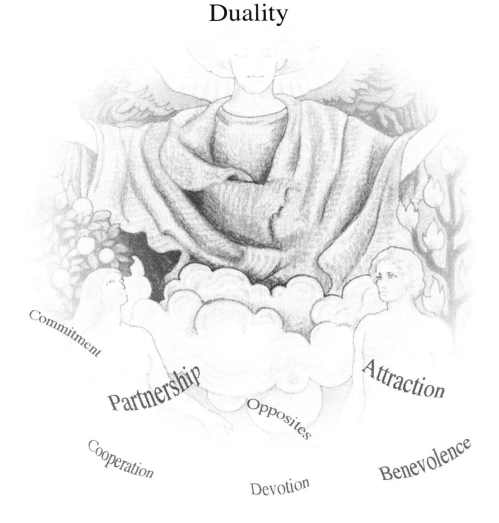

Commitment · Partnership · Opposites · Attraction
Cooperation · Devotion · Benevolence

The Chariot VII

Possible Meaning
~ Ability ~

Successful venture. Control over matters of concern. Great accomplishment.

A confident individual.

Progress on a goal.

Moving forward from a good position.

Advancement on a substantial objective.

The advantage is seen clearly on a goal and action taken swiftly.

An insurmountable force.

Key turning point for the better. Strong position. Having the advantage.

Taking control of a difficult situation. The ability to control influential powers. Unstoppable progress moving forward.

The vehicle of the self. Taking on challenges. In control of the situation you seek to be part of.

Being in tune with destiny.

Unbeatable if action is taken at the correct time.

Finding Meaning in the Cards 95

Crossing Barriers

Swiftness · Resourceful · Advancement · Well Executed
An Advantage

The Chariot VII
Ability

Swift Movement

Confidence

Efficiency

Courage · Experienced · Effortless · Quick Progress

Strength VIII

Possible Meaning
~ Fortitude ~

In touch with your higher self. Taking control. Overcoming temptation. Harmonious communication.

Control of the ego and animal instincts. Nourishing restraint. Fiery animal instincts.

Domesticated control of a situation. A keen understanding of the problem at hand.

Patience with a difficult situation.

Control coming from a strong position.

Trusted guidance.

This card can signify finding the right approach to the situation through gentle but forceful control.

A spiritual connection to our physical environment.

Mind, body and spirit working in perfect harmony.

Having the will to control and balance both sides of thought with gentle persuasion.

In a good position to take control.

Enchantment

Potential
Taming Free Will Challenging
Discipline

Strength VIII
Fortitude

Impact
Self Awareness
Inner Strength Control
Restraint Breaking Barriers
Moderation

The Hermit IX

Possible Meaning
~ Seclusion ~

A seeker of knowledge. The inner journey. Seeing things from a higher perspective.

Self-knowledge. Inner searching. Isolated enlightenment.

Disassociation. A need to break away from the pack. Looking within self for the answers. Soul searching.

Finding your true identity. In a good position for new awareness.

Understanding more than most. Standing alone on a viewpoint or opinion. In a space of clear vision. Keen insight on the situation.

Breaking away from the rest and going it alone.

A fulfilling quest is followed.

In a higher position to understand a particular viewpoint.

On a quest that must be taken alone.

At a higher level than before.

A new undertaking.

Finding Meaning in the Cards 99

Wisdom

Centering   Inner Searching   A Quest
True Path   Solitude

The Hermit IX
Seclusion

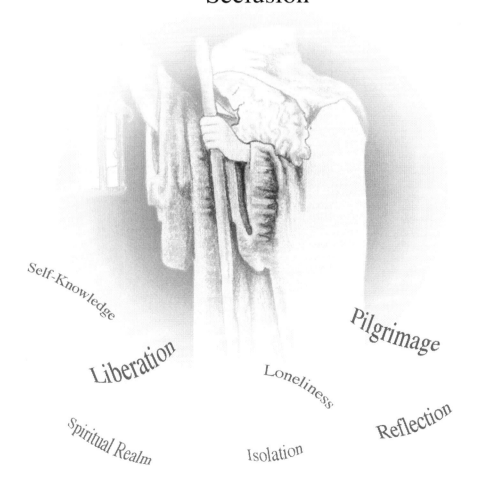

Self-Knowledge   Pilgrimage
Liberation   Loneliness   Reflection
Spiritual Realm   Isolation

The Wheel X

Possible Meaning
~ Destiny ~

The Wheel of Fortune represents moving on.

Advancement of a necessary cycle. Evolvement. The inevitable result to come.

Things are in motion. Finding the center of an issue.

Movement in directions good or bad.

Situations not in your control. Things set in motion. Predictable cycles. Foreseeable forecast.

Fate versus free will. Swayed by predestined mind-sets. Equilibrium. Progress on an objective is seen clearly.

Probability is in your favor. Lady Luck is close by. Continuous movement on a project at hand.

A time to prepare for your calling is close with opportunity to succeed.

As things move forward on your goal many changes are still to come. A time to prepare for an unpredictable opportunity.

Things are set in motion.

Finding Meaning in the Cards

Evolution

Destiny Unlocked Prediction Timeless
Opportunity

The Wheel X
Destiny

Precision
Your Calling Turn of Events Hopes and Dreams
Readiness In Motion Winds of Change

Justice XI

Possible Meaning
~ Balance ~

Universal truth and authority. Laws that can't be denied.

Clear facts based on reality. Balance of duality and polarity.

Undeniable conclusions.

Decisions are made based on truth.

Regulated justice. Sound opinions. A fair exchange of ideas. Rightful ownership. Justice restored. Decisions carefully thought through.

Decisions made with prudence. An act of fairness. Neutrality is a strong influence. A sense of satisfaction with accomplishments.

Decisions out of your control are finalized.

A sense of poise and integrity. All things will be seen clearly as the issue progresses.

Motive and purpose will be clearly understood as time moves forward.

Adjustment

Order · *Virtue* · *Universal Laws* · *Grace* · *Redemption*

Justice XI
Balance

Rightful · *Compensation* · *Equilibrium* · *Caution* · *Fairness* · *Innocence* · *Dignity*

The Hanged Man XII
Possible Meaning
~ Sacrifice ~

Principle is key.
Against the majority.

Seeing things from a different viewpoint than most. A radical position.

Sacrifice for strong views. High price for strong beliefs is paid.

A time of suspension. Unorthodox concepts are criticized.

Abandonment of a cause.
A time to let things pass. A reversal of ideas.

Seeing truth where others do not. Standing up for a principle others may not agree on.

Being in limbo and no movement at this time.

Ideas move forward, but they move slowly. A time of silence and inaction. Reflection can bring new ideas on your goal. Looking at things from a different light can reveal new insight.

Finding Meaning in the Cards 105

Initiation

Limited
Radical View Opposed Thinking In Limbo

The Hanged Man XII
Sacrifice

Consequences
Unorthodox
Strong Belief
Hidden Agenda
Reversal
Exposure
A Twist
New Direction

Death XIII

Possible Meaning
~ Deceased ~

You have to admit that this card is a little dramatic. I mean come on! So I just couldn't resist adding this EXTRA page for the Death card.
Intuitively, this card makes me think of.....DEATH!
I mean does this image seem like anything else? A skeleton on a horse. Dead people laying around in the card and all that?

See how dangerous Tarot cards can be? But you wanted a reading anyway. Oh well –you knew this card was in there somewhere. So now you are acting all surprised that it came up in your reading.

So, lets see if we can see this card in a more metaphorical sense.

Nah! Death is a pretty strong message.

I really do feel this card is a little dramatic for today's Tarot decks. Just my personal feeling. So don't take this interpretation literally. I just couldn't resist.
Besides, this is my book anyway.

Hey! All of a sudden I don't feel so good. I think my brain aneurysm is acting up again. Feel so weak!.....

I must...............finish..boooook........

Finding Meaning in the Cards 107

```
SURGEON GENERAL'S WARNING:
 Getting this card in a reading
    can cause serious illness
```

Death XIII
Oh No!

Does this look infected to you?

Can I have all your stuff?

That pesky anthrax!

Knock knock.
Who's there?
Not you anymore

Do you always look like this?

You might accidentally slip into a pool of pirahna

How old are you again?!

Don't buy any green bananas

Call 911!

Death XIII

Possible Meaning
~ Transition ~

Major transformation.

A cleansing of old issues. Purification is for the best.

Harvest.

A time for reflection on what has passed.

A new cycle of necessary changes. Acceptance of the inevitable.

End of one cycle and the beginning of the next. Reaping of old beliefs to make way for the new.

The end of familiar surroundings. A time to reap and make way for future growth.

Making ready for predictable situations to come.

A surrender to a higher cause. Liberating old thinking and making way for new ideas. A major transformation can create new awareness on your journey.

A necessary evolvement on an issue will create a better situation than before.

A time of progression. New growth.

Finding Meaning in the Cards

Cycles

Cleansing Harvest Purification Closure

Threshold

Death XIII
Transition

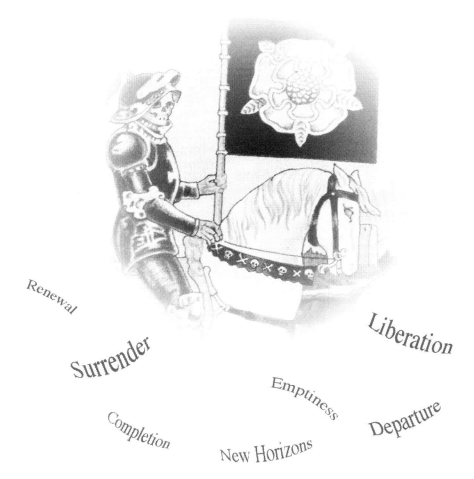

Renewal Surrender Emptiness Liberation Departure

Completion New Horizons

Temperance XIV

Possible Meaning
~ Inspiration ~

Following one's true passion. Inspiring forces are close by. Self control is key for the quest at hand.

Moderation and desire are balanced.

Great rewards and awareness.

Easy flow of ideas. Coordinating harmony with efforts being made.

Effective results are accomplished through an even keel way of thinking.

Levelheaded and steadfast actions will bring good results.

Smooth transformation while keeping balance and harmony.

Staying on the middle path and avoiding extremes.

Working in harmony with others. Inspiration is strong.

Finding Meaning in the Cards 111

Equilibrium

Rewarding
Bliss High Values Protector
Honored

Temperance XIV
Inspiration

Steadfast
Gratification Having Purpose Guardianship
Centered Care Giver Worthy Quest

The Devil XV

Possible Meaning
~ False Fears ~

Not seeing the truth. Believing false truths. Looking in the wrong direction.

Darkness and self-doubt. Vulnerable to deception.
In a space of darkness. A time to watch for falling backwards instead of advancing forward.

Twisted truths. Dark influence.

Allowing things to be put off until a later date that should be addressed. Seclusion and secrecy about actions taken. Untrusting and dwelling in remorse.

Stalling and deceiving self on a situation. Weak excuses are easily found. A time to focus on positive actions.

Stuck in a self-destructive manner or habit. A time to break away from negative routines and create a better situation.

Disregard for other's feelings and concerns limits your progress.

Finding Meaning in the Cards

Ignorance

Denial Excuses Procrastination Obsession
Half-Truths

The Devil XV
False Fears

Self Pity Dependency Closed-Minded Pettiness Deception
Manipulation Hateful

The Tower XVI

Possible Meaning
~ Disruption ~

Disruption. Change of plans. New direction is needed.

Abrupt change. A need to watch for surprise and the unexpected.

A time to prepare for challenges to come. An unfamiliar environment.

A breakthrough on a challenge. Abrupt change brings some confusion. A time to make ready for the unexpected.

Preparation is a good choice.

Things taken for granted are lost if they are not looked after with more detail.

Seeking alliance with others on your concern. Change will bring about challenges.

Intense influence from an outside source not in your control.

A falling away of old ideas.

Walls of resistance are broken down.

Finding Meaning in the Cards

Intervention

Unprepared   Threatening   Challenges
Delays   In Jeopardy

The Tower XVI
Disruption

A Test
Vulnerability   Precaution   Abrupt Change
Initiation   Accountability   Unexpected

The Star XVII

Possible Meaning
~ Direction ~

A clear point of reference is seen. Actions are taken in a good direction.

Clear passage is still to be taken. Signs from outside influences are seen with favor.

A balance of logic and intuition is used well.

Hopeful outcome.

Progress on your chosen path.

A peaceful setting after the storm.

Moving in a positive direction. Answers are found and action taken.

Signs are seen for good direction. Help from an unknown source brings new insight.

Plans are good to move forward on your quest. Staying on course with a plan well thought through will bring rewards and success.

Time is right to take action on your goal. Good balance in place to shift in positive ways to an end.

Finding Meaning in the Cards

New Vision

Faith
On Course Knowing Revealing Drawn To

The Star XVII
Direction

Hope
Guidance A Message Destination
Trust Preparation Well Grounded

The Moon XVIII

Possible Meaning
~ Mysterious Paths ~

Intuitive and imaginative thinking.

Hidden and mysterious messages.

Unknown destiny on your path at this time. Not clearly seen. Objectives are vague.

A time of illusion. The unexplored aspects of a quest still to be discovered.

A time to follow your intuition.

Path is dimly lit. A time to look deep within intuitive insight. Lunar cycles could be a key factor.

A time to confront what is unseen. Reflection can be an illusion. A time to move cautiously on your quest.

More needs to be known before proceeding at a faster pace. Sure-footed movement is wise at this time.

More will be understood in time as you proceed on this goal.

Moving forward with no sense of clear direction is not wise.

Finding Meaning in the Cards 119

Tranquil Crossroad

The Moon XVIII
Mysterious Paths

Hidden · Instinctual · Unexplored · Imagination · Lost · Portals · Illumination · Enchantment · Illusion · Reluctance · Crossroads · The Unknown

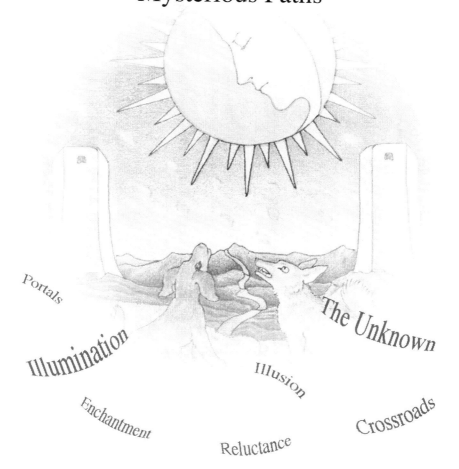

The Sun XIX

Possible Meaning
~ Nurturing ~

A nurturing situation.

New light shed on old viewpoints.

Seeing things clearly. Bright cleansing of issues.

Lifegiving source. Outside influences are positive.

Bright future. In a good position to influence others nearby.

Shedding light on the subject comes easy at this time.

Centering of issues creates balance for all involved.

A complete understanding of the issue at hand. Clear guidance from a reliable source.

A warm and secure outcome. A new start.

Issues causing shadows are easily detected and eliminated. All is out in the open.

An easy time to predict an outcome with accuracy.

Centered Focus

Renewal Expansion Clarity Warmth

Vibrance

The Sun XIX
Nurturing

Comfort

Healing

Safe Haven

New Life

Friendships Recovery Enlightening

Judgment XX

Possible Meaning
~ Awakening ~

A new understanding on an issue of concern.

Positive aspects are weighed against the negative and decisions are made.

A time to address truth. Actions are evaluated.

Credit is given for honorable deeds. Lifted to new heights of accomplishment.

Your calling is heard from the heart. Evolvement on an issue is creating a major shift within the situation at hand.

An awakening of new interest in your quest is seen by others. New life in an old situation can be accomplished.

Your message is heard well by others.

Uplifting Devotion

Truth
Emerging
Enlightenment
Elevation
Uplifting

Judgement XX
Awakening

Promotion
Commencement
New Awareness
Realization
Summoned
A Calling
Accountability

The World XXI

Possible Meaning
~ Perfect Balance ~

A journey is complete.

Joy and celebration at the end of a completed quest.

Peaceful and perfect harmony.

Happy outcomes. New understanding of things not previously known.

A time of gratification and happiness. The end of a wonderful journey. Moving up another level.

All is seen with perfect understanding to a good ending on your quest. A time of happiness.

Celebration with those close to you. Balance on all aspects of a goal is accomplished.

Perfect balance. Concerns are addressed for all involved.

Confirmation of a successful venture. All is moving in perfect order as planned.

A time of joy and celebration.

Finding Meaning in the Cards

Perpetual Bliss

Unity

Joyful Tranquility Acceptance

Harmony

The World XXI
Perfect Balance

Devotion

Freedom Fulfillment

Journey's End Vitality Discovery

Understanding

Are you in for another chapter?

5. Working A Card Spread

THE CARD READING BROKEN DOWN:

THE OBJECTIVE:
The objective is something you plan to achieve.
The question being looked into during a reading is an objective.

THE STRATEGY:
The strategy is an accurate plan to achieve the objective.
The card spread is the blueprint of that plan. The map of the question. The more accurate the strategy is, the better the results towards that objective will be. A card spread is a strategy of an objective being looked into.

The rules for most strategies are few and simple. They can be learned in a week. But they are the most important part of the process. Breaking your question apart into it's basic elements is how strategies are done. The method for any logical analysis requires doing this.

THE TACTICS:
The tactics are the actual execution of the strategy.
The Tarot cards interpreted in a reading are the tactics used to accomplish the strategy of the card spread.

The card spread is the strategy and the Tarot cards placed into the spread and interpreted are the tactics used.

The Tarot cards are like the hammer and nails used to build a house. The card spread is the blueprint of that house being built.

The quality of my tools used to build that house are not as important as the accuracy of my blueprint.

The Tarot cards are the car driven to a destination.
The card spread is the road map to where you are driving to.

The make of car I drive to get where I want to go is not as important as the accuracy of the map I am using to reach that destination.

So whether I build my house using *Craftsman* tools or *Stanley* tools, I'd better have good blueprints.

Whether I drive a *Chevy* or a *Ford* to my destination, I'd better have good directions.

And whether I read Tarot cards using the *Tarot of Marseilles* or *Rider-Waite Tarot Deck* I'd better have a good understanding of how to look at questions I'm asked to find answers to. The card spread.

STRATEGIES:
Blueprints
Road maps
Card spreads.

TACTICS USED:
Craftsman or *Stanley* tools
Chevys or Fords
Tarot of Marseilles or *Rider-Waite Tarot Deck or any other Tarot deck.*

I think we spend too much time focusing on minute details of symbolism in various Tarot decks and not enough attention to the card spreads they are used in.

Good tactics won't get us far without a good strategy behind them.

The most important element of a card reading is the card spread itself. It is the map used to find answers and solutions.

A card spread is a way of asking the cards key points concerning our questions. A card spread is a collection of assumptions we seek to find answers to.

But have we really thought much about what kind of questions to ask the cards? A question can be seen from many angles and different viewpoints. Not just the obvious things that immediately come to mind.

Some of my card spreads have the positions interact with each other in a freestyle manner. Some of these spreads allow us to choose aspects of our question randomly – just like we choose the cards placed into those aspects randomly. This forces us to see our question from a different perspective than normally seen. A different viewpoint of our question we didn't consider before.

Average questions get average answers and will not help you find fresh ideas. To find some new way to see your question we need to ask more than typical questions.

We are not limited to following rigid procedures with card spreads. Normally if we don't like one card spread's meanings we choose one whose meanings seem to fit more in line with the questions we seek answers to. Isn't that like the tail wagging the dog? Why don't we just ask the cards what we want to ask them?

Card spreads positions usually keep the same meaning for every reading. I feel this could be changed. Think of the cards as an old friend. What would you ask that old friend about your question if the two of you were talking about it? Why don't we do that to create a specific card spread for each question asked?

The order cards are laid down, the pattern the spread creates on the table, and the strict unchangeable meanings for each position, are not necessary procedures.

What's important is the meanings those positions have towards our question. Are they useful meanings? If not, we can make them useful to our questions. The choice is up to us.

The main curve ball is that we never really see the card spread. We only see the cards laid into it. *Out of sight – out of mind*. But the card spread does exist. It is the main component of the process.

If we look at this invisible thing called a card spread closer we can see there is much we can do with it to improve our readings. All we ever see are the cards laid into it.

The positions of the card spread – the questions asked – are invisible on our table. The cards and the card spread are separate parts of the process. Just like a question is separate from an answer. The spread is a series of questions. The cards are placed into those questions as possible answers. I feel that is why the Tarot's knack to work has remained a mystery for so long. No one ever sees the spread on the table. They just see the cards laid into it.

The secret of the Tarot's ability as a successful application is something we never really see – the card spread.

And when answers are found, what do we look at with amazement? – The cards. We look at those cards, and only those cards. We never consider how they were used as the source of insight we found in the reading.

THE CARD SPREADS

I would like to start by showing the Horseshoe spread. The Horseshoe spread is one many professionals use and has been around a long time as a classic. The Celtic Cross is another spread in this chapter that I feel is very useful and is what I usually use to read professionally.

The rest of the spreads here are all original and you won't find them anywhere else but on these pages. They are more interactive types of spreads that can be read from many different angles. I feel that makes for a more effective spread and can show more possibilities to consider for ideas; possible solutions and answers.

I wanted to break away from ordered and structured type card spreads. I thought it would be useful to have card spreads whose positions can interact with each other to see new aspects of a question asked.

I will start out by showing the Horseshoe spread the way it's always done. Then I will show another version of the same spread using a popular creative thinking technique known as SCAMPER. You will see that both use the same creative thinking techniques. The position meanings are the only thing that changes. Otherwise they are identical applications.

The only difference is the Tarot card reader would usually use the typical Horseshoe spread and the Creative Consultant would usually use the Scamper type spread. I did this to show you how similar creative thinking and Tarot card readings really are.

Mapping the Question
Traditional Horseshoe Card Spread

Seeing Yourself

4

Hidden Influences

3

Outside Influences

5

The Present

2

Opportunities

6

The Past

1

The Prediction

7

Reading the Map
Traditional Horseshoe Card Spread

The seven elements of the Horseshoe spread are meant to be read individually. Then the information that is seen is combined to create meaning in relation to your question.

Position #1. The past in relation to the question. The history of the question and how does any of the past help me find answers and solutions.

Position #2. The present and how it relates to your question. The immediate situation as it currently stands. Searching for actions that can be currently taken in our favor before opportunity is lost.

Position #3. Hidden influences are considered in this position. Are there things that could be affecting the situation that haven't been considered? Are you seeing all important aspects of the situation?

Position #4. This position allows us to look closely at ourselves and what we are really trying to achieve. Why do we want this? What is our motive?

Position #5. This position allows us to look at the things that seem out of our control? Outside influences. Is there any way we can control any of these outside influences?

Position #6. Here we look for any hint of opportunity that could help us achieve our objective. This could be anything from people to events that we could look at as possible advantages not previously seen.

Position #7. This position is to help us find a final message and direction to our objective. It is used in combination with the rest of the reading to finding a prediction. A plan to accomplish success.

If a negative card is placed in position #7 it is something we can look to avoid. Something to watch for. A warning to keep in mind as we proceed.

Mapping the Question
SCAMPER – Creative Thinking Technique

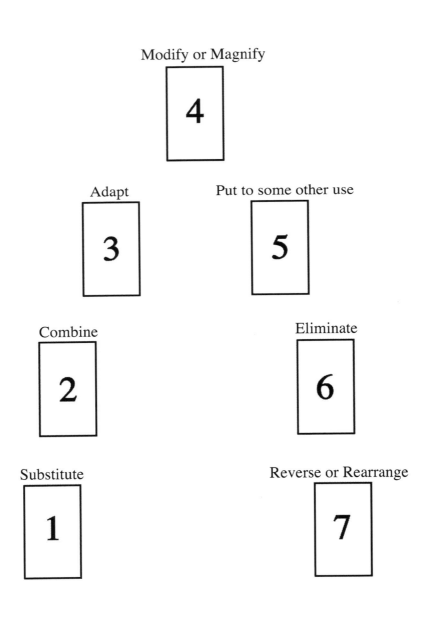

SCAMPER – Creative Thinking Technique

SCAMPER is probably one of the most common creative thinking techniques out there. Here you will see how using it is exactly the same as the card reader's technique. The pattern the cards are laid in isn't important. The elements could be just laid out left to right instead of a horseshoe. What's important is the elements being looked into in regards to the question. The word SCAMPER comes from the elements used.

S. Position #1. What can be *substituted* to put things in your favor?

C. Position #2. What can be *combined* to help this be successful?

A. Position #3. What can be *adapted* to this idea for an answer?

M. Position #4. How can this be *modified* in some way. Or *magnified*?

P. Position #5. Can this idea be *put to another use*? Something better?

E. Position #6. What can be *eliminated* to help the issue work?

R. Position #7. Can things be *rearranged* to fit better? *Reversed*?

The creative thinker would add a random stimulus to each position to spark ideas. Randomness added to positions forces us to look at our question in new ways for answers. To see things we didn't previously see.

The creative consultant uses anything in the world to be placed into elements of the question to spark ideas. From random words from the page of a book to things you might find in a hardware store. Anything, including Tarot cards could be used.

The technique of adding randomness is commonly known as Conceptual Blending and is done by both applications shown here.

The Tarot card reader limits their random source to a deck of 78 Tarot cards. The creative thinker uses anything in the world around them.

The Rings of Saturn Spread

The Rings of Saturn spread is meant to bombard you with an array of random aspects to choose from. You will need to get a deck of playing cards that are no longer being used. Take 18 of the playing cards and write down the number and key word of each of the 18 positions on the 18 playing cards. Example would be the first card would have *#1 Feasibility* written on it. The second card would have *#2 Eliminate* written on it. And so on.

Now you have a complete deck of 18 element cards that can be randomly selected to look into a question with. Shuffle the 18 cards and lay out a number of the cards. You decide how big a card spread you want to use. Randomly laying out 3 of the 18 element cards would create a three card spread. Laying out 6 random element cards would create a 6 card spread and so on. These become the positions of your card spread. Next place a Tarot card to each position to be interpreted for ideas.
Or you can just read this as an 18-card spread as shown in the diagram.

What the Elements Propose:
#1– What makes this question *Feasible*?
#2– What can be *Eliminated* in this question to help find a solution?
#3– What can be *Magnified* about this question?
#4– What is the real *Purpose* of this objective?
#5– How can I *Adapt* something else to this issue?
#6– Are there any *Patterns* here that may help me see a solution?

#7– Can I *Rephrase* the question in a better way?
#8– Are there any *Obligations* that will interfere with advancing forward?
#9– Is there some order of things that would help if I *Reverse* them?
#10– Can something be *Combined* with it to help create a solution?
#11– Can something be *Substituted* to create a better situation?
#12– What can be done to create a *Win-Win* situation to this question?

#13– Is there some *History* about this question that might help to look at?
#14– What are the *Rewards* about pursuing this objective?
#15– How can I *Initiate* a new incentive to move this forward?
#16– What *Opportunities* are possible to move forward on this question?
#17– What can we *Predict* to happen at this time that can help us?
#18– Is there a specific *Location* ideal to act on this question?

Working a Card Spread   137

The Rings of Saturn Spread

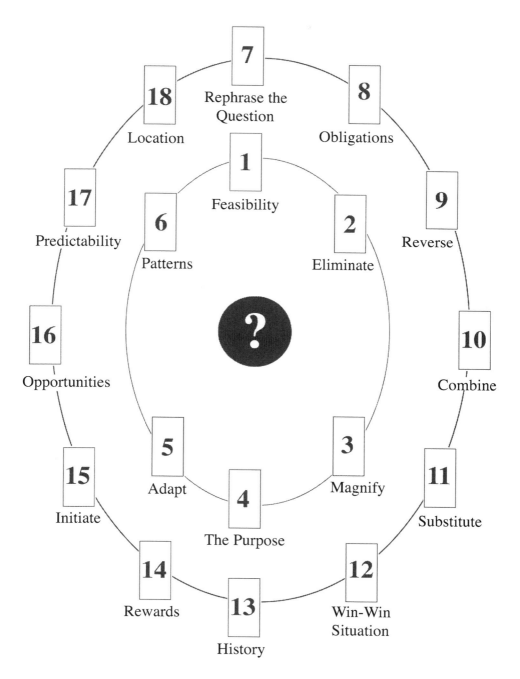

The Rings of Saturn Spread

Example:

I decided to do a 4 card spread in this example. The cards I drew were #8 Obligations – #10 Combine – #4 The Purpose – #16 Opportunities.

#8 – Are there any *Obligations* that will interfere with moving forward?
#10– Can things be *Combined* with my question to create a solution?
#4– What is the real *Purpose* of this objective?
#16– What *Opportunities* are possible to move forward on this question?

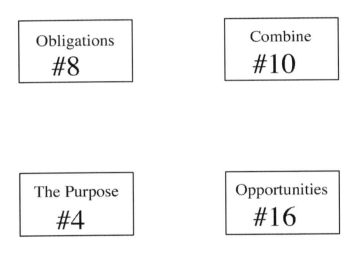

So these are the four aspects we will look into in regards to my question. Whatever that question happens to be is not important to explain how this spread works.

Random positions to a question allow us to look at our question in ways we might not normally consider.

Now we will lay Tarot cards with these four position cards to spark ideas. A random stimulus application is used for both the positions and the cards laid into them.

The Rings of Saturn Spread
Example:

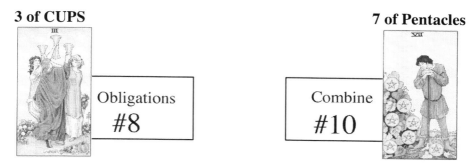

3 of Cups — Creativity
• What new ideas can I create that will help keep my *obligations* from interfering as I pursue this issue?

7 of Pentacles — Confidence
• What aspects of my question do I feel confident about to *combine* in some way to make things more favorable?

Page of Pentacles — New Path
• How do I see the *purpose* of this issue as a new beginning for me? How do I benefit from this new direction?

High Priestess II — Mystery
• What *opportunities* am I not seeing yet? What elements of this issue still seem mysterious that I need to know more about? If I focus on finding answers to those mysteries, would they become new *opportunities*?

Sun Tzu's Gate

The Sun Tzu's Gate spread is named after the military genius Sun Tzu. The positions can be read in order or they can be read in ways that interact with each other. This spread is good for situations where something is resisting or blocking you. Whether the obstacle is a person or an issue, these factors are useful to find answers.

The eight aspects to this spread work well for understanding your strengths, your weaknesses, and seeing a promising way to achieve your objective. The spread also goes into the aspects of something blocking your objective. It looks at the strengths and weaknesses of that resistance working against you. That resistance can be a specific person or a general obstacle or challenge of some type.

The 1st position allows us to take a close look at ourselves.

The 2nd position allows us to look and try to understand the challenge that is working against us.

The 3rd position is an opportunity to see our own strengths.

The 4th position is an opportunity to see our challenge's strengths.

The 5th position helps us find a way to successful action.

The 6th position allows us to look for a way to misdirect our challenge's strengths away from our weaknesses.

The 7th position helps me protect or strengthen my weaknesses.

The 8th position allows me to focus on weak or vulnerable aspects my challenge has that I might be able to take advantage of.

Working a Card Spread   141

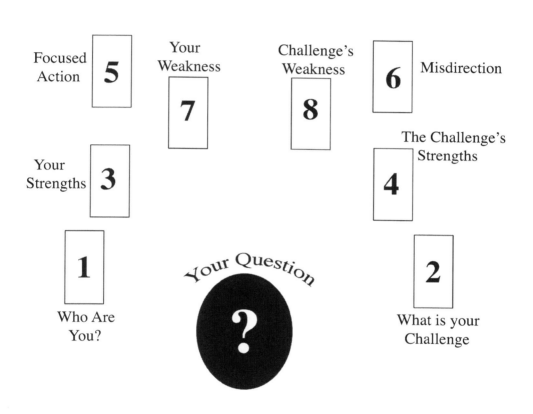

Sun Tzu's Gate

The positions for this spread can be read in numerical order or they can be read in ways that interact with each other. An example can be seen with Misdirect #6 – my challenge's strengths #4 – away from my weaknesses #7.

Conceptually blending the randomness of a Tarot card to each position helps spark new ideas to these issues that we wouldn't normally see.

Some say Sun Tzu's teachings hold the victory to life's quests.
His book *The Art of War* was from around 500 BC. It is used today by many to succeed. From governments and sports teams to Fortune 500 companies. These 8 aspects of his teachings are a basic part of his work.

Sun Tzu's Gate

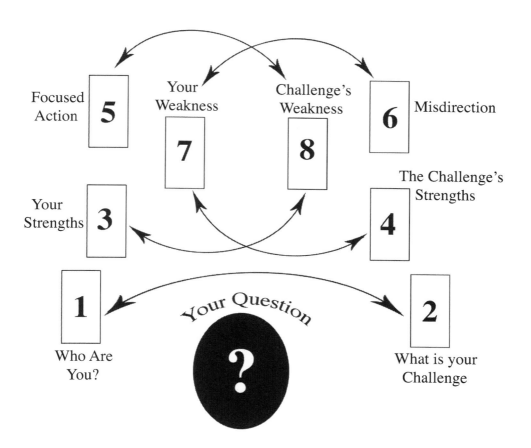

The Celtic Cross

I feel that the Celtic Cross is a great spread to learn with. I have put it in my last two books and I'm continuing on with this one. Here, I want to use it to show how card spreads can be performed with more specific insight.

I feel that we tend to look at the positions of a card spread as unchangeable.

What I like to look at in the Celtic Cross is seeing the real question at hand. What is currently being done. What is the client trying to achieve. The purpose of this goal. Assets the client has. Opportunities for the client and a prediction.

I always use the Celtic Cross when I do professional readings.
This is the way I've done the Celtic Cross for over 20 years.

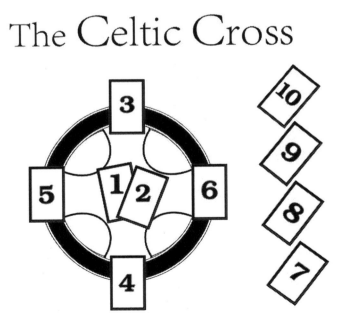

Positions #1 & #2: The question itself —

These two positions are meant to be an in-depth look into the question we seek to find answers to. This is a look at the question itself.

In what way can these two cards give me new ways to see my objective more clearly? Can I rephrase my question into something with more clarity. How can these cards help me see the real question I seek to find answers to? A direct look at the question itself is important. Therefore two cards are used in this portion of the spread instead of one.

Position #3: Currently Going Through —

Position three allows us to question the actions we are currently taking in attempting to achieve our objective. Am I doing anything the wrong way? Are my efforts working? Is there some way of changing my efforts in a way that will get better results toward my goal? What does this card show me that can be applied for positive actions to take place? Am I doing too much? Am I doing unnecessary work? Is what I'm doing getting me anywhere? Is there some other action I should be taking instead of the ones I'm currently involved with?

Position #4: Trying to Achieve —

Position four allows us to look into what it is we are trying to achieve. It allows us to question what it is we want from this. Why am I putting so much effort in position #3 to reach position #4? What is the reasoning behind getting this in my life. What does this card show me that makes clear what I'm ultimately trying to accomplish?

Position #5: An Asset —

Position five allows us to focus on an asset we have in our corner that can help us achieve the goal. What does this card show you as far as assets you have that you are not utilizing yet? What does this card show you about yourself that you have overlooked, that can help you accomplish this goal? Can this card show you where you might be selling yourself short on some type of talent or resource you've overlooked about yourself?

Position #6: An Opportunity to come —

This position allows us to look into possible opportunities that will be coming in the near future. What does this card show you in relation to anticipated events, meetings or some other future interaction? What can the card see as far as a coming together of opposing influences that might be resolved if preparation is made? Can your asset from position #5 help when this opportunity arises?

Position #7: The clients perception of their own question —

Sometimes we can get stuck seeing our question from only one viewpoint. You might be seeing a positive thing in a negative way or a negative thing in a positive light. You might be seeing this question as a stuck situation and needing to leave it. Your attitude might be affecting what is really happening with this situation. What does this card tell you about the way you're seeing your own question? Are you seeing things correctly?

Position #8: The Timing —

How we take timing into consideration can have important results. Is it time to evaluate a situation? A time to act on it? A time to let things rest? A time for reconciliations? What does this card tell you about how to act at this time about your question? Time to wait? Or time to act before opportunity is lost?

Position #9: The Purpose —

Unlike position #4, *Trying to Achieve* – Position #9 is the big picture. What we are ultimately trying to achieve. An example of this might be trying to achieve a promotion at work because I want to make more money. Why? The purpose might be I want to provide better for my family. This can be good to look into because it's so big that many feel it is just assumed as the reason why I want this in my life. So asking what is the real purpose can bring about enlightening awareness to the client themselves about their actions and what they are really trying to accomplish.

Position #10: The Prediction —

This position helps us wrap up the reading. As we recap everything, what does this card show us to help fine tune things? If it's a negative card it can show things to watch for as you move forward. A positive card here shows things should move easily as you proceed.

Here is where you make your predictions and give insight on the best ways to proceed.

Putting more meaning into the positions like this makes it easier to see meaning in the cards for answers.

In the next example we will go back to the Horseshoe spread and do the same thing. The meanings of the positions will all be based on four elements. Those elements are WHAT, WHY, HOW and WHEN for each position.

I feel WHAT, WHY, HOW and WHEN can be helpful to any question being looked into. If we keep them in mind as we read, the answers can be seen clearly.

148 Radical Tarot - Breaking All the Rules

Traditional Horseshoe Card Spread
Deeper Position Meaning

Seeing Yourself

4

Hidden Influences   Outside Influences

3   **5**

The Present   Opportunities

2   **6**

The Past   The Prediction

1   **7**

Traditional Horseshoe Card Spread
with deeper position meaning

Detailed Positions:

Most sources on the Tarot will show a lengthy description for the card definitions. These are usually three or four sentences of meaning for each card. Some works might give a full page to define a card's meaning. These same sources will go the opposite direction when it comes to defining the card spread positions. These are usually one or two words to describe the meaning of each position in the card spread.

As you saw in my chapter on card meanings, I like one or two words to define a card's meaning; called key-word meaning. But I feel the various positions of a card spread is where detailed description is best used. So, key-word meanings for the card definitions and three or four sentence definitions for the card spread positions gives us another twist to the application of the card reading. Remember that the positions are the questions asked. The cards give us possible answers. Here the card positions have many aspects of the position in question using *What, Why, How* and *When* as aspects of each position.

See if placing a Tarot card into these positions can help create new insight into the question. If the card can help just one of those aspects it can make a big difference towards your final goal's success.

THE PAST #1:

First position is looking into the past of the situation.

What can the past tell us about the situation? What patterns are seen that we can anticipate happening again?

Why have these things happened in the past on this issue? What can we do to avoid them happening again? If they are good, what can we do to continue those things happening again? How does the past help me achieve what I'm trying to accomplish? Does the past have any history of successful results in regard to this situation? When in the past did the timing affect the situation in a positive way? Can I make this happen again? How about in a negative way? Can I avoid that happening again?

THE PRESENT #2:

The second position looks at the present on the situation.

What is the present situation? Is it different than the past?

Or is there no change. Is it stagnant? Or is it peaceful?

What are we currently doing about the situation? Why? What is the purpose we are trying to achieve at this time? How is the best way to proceed for the best results right now? What factors can we focus on at the present time regarding this situation?

HIDDEN INFLUENCES #3:

What are the present influences I might not be seeing? How can I align them to work in my favor? Are there any influences I haven't considered? Hidden? Things I'm not seeing clearly that might be affecting the outcome? Why are these outside influences around? Can I deter them if they are working against me? Can I make them more prevalent if they are working for me?

How can I take more control of the influences surrounding the question? How can I get them to work more for me and not against me? When is the right time to take action on these influences? Will time change the influences in some way? Do these influences work in cycles that can be anticipated in the future?

SEEING YOURSELF #4:

What is my involvement with this situation? What am I capable of doing? Can I do more? What are my strengths? Can I use them in some way for this situation? What are my weaknesses? Can I deter them being exposed in this situation? Why do I want this in my life?

How can I see myself as a positive influence in this situation? Is there something expected of me? Is it really what I should be doing? Is this the right time for me to be involved with this challenge? Would I be in a better position on this issue if I wait?

OUTSIDE INFLUENCES #5:

What outside influences are involved in this issue?
Are they directly a part of this? Why are they involved? What is their interest in being a part of this issue?

How can these outside influences be used to better the situation? If they are negative influences, how can they be substituted with positive influences. When is the best time to act to convince these influences to align with your way of thinking?

OPPORTUNITIES #6:

What opportunities are seen on this issue? What is needed to succeed on this issue? Is there opportunity for that to happen? Why is the opportunity here? What is the reason the opportunity makes itself available? Its purpose?

How do I go about achieving a successful outcome with this opportunity? Does this opportunity want something from me as return?
Is there a time when the opportunity is more easily swayed in my favor? What is the best way to handle this opportunity to my best advantage?

PREDICTION #7:

What is the purpose of this objective? What will it bring me if it comes to pass. How will I benefit from this if it is successful? Why do I want this prediction to come to pass?

How can I best make this prediction happen? What can I do to make this opportunity even more predictable in my favor? What is the time element on this prediction? Is the timing advantageous? Can the timing be altered to a better date?

Random Tarot Cards:

Now lay a card into each of these seven positions and see if it can help with any of these questions. If one new aspect is found, it can create a whole new scenario to the situation's outcome.

The cards will give us answers. But first we need to have useful questions to be answered. If the questions are vague, the answers will be vague as well. In-depth card positions allow us to see our questions with more detail. This helps the cards find useful answers to one or more of the aspects asked in each position.

How to create aspects of a card spread

Create specific meanings for each card position

Creating a set of elements to be used in card spreads isn't that difficult. Create a set of assumptions that pertain to your question. To your goal. Ask what you want to know about.

Card spreads are usually viewed as static. Not changing from one question to another. If I use the Celtic Cross for a reading with Mary who is asking about a relationship or Joe who is asking about a career move, the position meanings remain the same for both. I feel ignoring that restriction opens up the reading to clearer messages of insight and ideas. Position meanings can be custom fit to elements of a question if you choose to do that.

Position meanings can pertain to a specific person or a specific project. They are just aspects of a question being looked into. The questions the positions represent can become very distinct and precise if you change them to fit the question more closely.

Create random position meanings

Just like the Tarot cards that are used in a reading are selected randomly, so can the positions be selected in the same manner. Randomly. This forces us to see aspects about our question we might not normally think about asking. Random meanings can open up many ideas about your question.

The Rings of Saturn spread earlier in this chapter shows one example of this. Random positions force us to look at aspects of our question we might not normally consider thinking about.

You could create your own Rings of Saturn type of spread with all new random elements. You are not limited to just 18 elements as well. The possibilities are endless.

What is a Tarot Card reading?

I would like to show how breaking a subject apart into sections is a universal method of analysis. No matter what it is we're looking into, it is a basic strategy to clearly understand what it is you are trying to know more about. Obviously, Tarot cards are not a good fit for every concept we want to understand more about in our lives. But mapping our question into segments remains consistent with anything we look into as the strategy we use to understand more about something.

Here we are looking into the game of chess. The game of chess would never have any reason to consult the Tarot cards. But if we wanted to learn how to play the game, breaking the subject apart into sections becomes useful. In anything we are looking to understand it is a basic strategy to break it apart into sections. Reading Tarot cards follows that same basic principle. We call it the card spread. This is a necessary part to understanding whatever we are trying to learn more about. Whether it's a card reading or learning chess the procedure remains the same. It is the way our mind naturally works.

The Game of Chess as an example

Here are the basics aspects of learning how to play the game of chess.

Aspect #1 is King safety.
Aspect #2 is Material advantage
Aspect #3 is The Center
Aspect #4 is Development
Aspect #5 is Mobility
Aspect #6 is Open lines

We can see the six aspects of this example on chess strategy as the same application as a Tarot card spread. The six aspects of consideration now become positions to the question of chess. A card spread works the same way.

It's a valuable way of seeing clearly what it is we're trying to understand, whatever the subject happens to be.

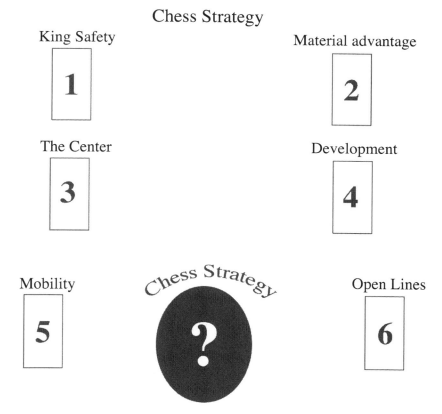

How we go about learning more about a subject isn't important. Whether we read books on the subject of chess or we consult Tarot cards about some issue to spark ideas – breaking the question into sections is key.

The card spread is a basic but important part of the process to reading Tarot cards. This type of analysis is vital to anything we wish to understand more about. I wanted to show how important this part of a card reading really is. In anything we are looking to understand, it is a basic strategy to break it apart into sections.

This is an effective and common way to look at any subject or question to learn more about it. And we do this with a Tarot card reading. We call it a card spread. Aspects of a question being looked into.

This is a very useful way to look at a question. To analyze it. It works better than using an outline type format. Using an outline format is great when we want to relay information we already know to other people. But when we are looking to find answers ourselves it won't get you too far. To find new ideas to something we need a map. A card reading is a verbally expressed mind-map.

Getting new ideas:

If there are no sources of information available to the aspects of our question, if our mind can't find solutions, we need to spark a new source for ideas. We have to go beyond what we know. We need new ideas or our mind will remain stuck in thinking patterns that are not going to get us anywhere on the subject. Our mind will keep snapping back to answers that aren't working for us. We become stuck in old thinking patterns.

This is when Conceptual Blending is useful to find new ideas. Once you have a question, break it apart into sections. Then, when you need new ideas to those aspects of your question, add a random stimulus of any kind. If you like to use the Tarot cards, they work really well for this. Our mind will search those cards to stimulate new ideas for answers for each aspect of a question they are blended with.

The Tarot cards have been and remain a great Conceptual Blending tool.

Conceptual Blending:

CONCEPTUAL BLENDING Defined:
Conceptual blending refers to a set of cognitive operations for combining (or **blending**) words, images, and ideas in a network of "mental spaces" to create **meaning**. Also known as **conceptual** integration theory.

Conceptual blending, also called conceptual integration or view application, is a theory of cognition developed by Gilles Fauconnier and Mark Turner. According to this theory, elements and vital relations from diverse scenarios are "blended" in a subconscious process, which is assumed to be ubiquitous to everyday thought and language. Conceptual blending is an emerging field of studies for computer scientists wishing to pursue research in artificial intelligence.
– From Wikipedia

Conceptual blending combines a random dissimilar subject to a segment of a question being looked into to force new thoughts about that question.

Adding something remotely different to your subject will force a connection between the two. Your imagination will find a way to connect the dots – to blend —in some way that makes sense to you. Your mind will naturally search for similarities between the two subjects no matter how dissimilar the two subjects happen to be.

Your mind does this all on its own without any real training.

Anything ever created, great or small, was done by adding something we are totally familiar with to the subject we are trying to find an answer to and blending them together for new ideas.

Becoming familiar with the Tarot cards allows you to use them specifically as a conceptual blending tool to find answers to things you are not familiar with. To things you don't initially have an answer to.

The best way to shake up old thinking patterns is to throw in a new, seemingly unrelated element. The mind will work overtime trying to fit it into that pattern — until it alters the pattern.

This is what we do when we search for a meaning a Tarot card can have in relation to an issue being looked into. We search for ways that card can suggest ideas to be associated to the position in the card spread. And we find them.

Conceptual Blending is exactly what the Tarot reader does. The card reader blends a random card into a position of a card spread. The position represents a segment of our question. The random Tarot card placed into that position is interpreted to help find meaning. It forces our mind out of stuck thinking patterns and blends ideas to see something not thought of before.

Knowing and understanding this will change the way you read the Tarot.

The more you learn about creative thinking techniques and Conceptual Blending, the more you will see how it relates to a Tarot card reading.

The Tarot cards wouldn't help us learn the game of chess in any way at all. The topic of chess was just used to show how we should look at a question we are trying to understand more about. Learning chess can be mastered by using conventional thinking. Answers are available to learn all about it.

Creative thinking techniques are used for questions we are stuck in finding an answer to.

Crossing Positions

Something you can do with just the card spread positions without using the cards is cross one position over another to see how it can alter your perception of meaning to your question.

Here are a few examples:

1• Take one position element *from* another position element
2• Take one position element *through* another position element
3• Take one position element *above* another position element
4• Take one position element *opposite* another position element
5• Take one position element *while using* another position element
6• Take one position element *before using* another position element
7• Take one position element *so that* another position element
8• Take one position element *when* another position element
9• Take one position element *into* another position element
10• Take one position element *beyond* another position element
11• Take one position element *past* another position element

This is just another way of using card spread ideas before any cards are ever in play. Does it change anything at all?
See if this list of options works with one of your card spreads in some manner. It might show some new ideas for you.

An old spread from the 1960's

I doubt that anyone would use this spread today. But it shows how far we've come in 50 years. It was called "The Medium Draw." The Major and Minor cards were separated into separate packs. Major Arcana cards were placed in the upper arched part of the spread. Four cards for each category of Men, Women, and Children.

Then, the result card at the bottom of each category was always chosen from the Minor Arcana pack. This card was selected by adding up the numerical value of the Majors in that particular section you are reading —Men —Women —Child and then counting off the top of the Minor Arcana pack to that particular amount.

So if you get a number of 14 you would take the 14th card from the top of the pack of the Minor Arcana and place that into the result position to be read. That card would be interpreted as a result.

I think it's interesting that the old instruction manual I got this spread from referred to reading the Tarot cards as "HOW TO PLAY TAROT." Again, we didn't have much information to work with back then. No wonder these cards were considered mysterious! There wasn't really much else as far as info on how to do this spread. You just did it.

The Medium Draw Card Spread

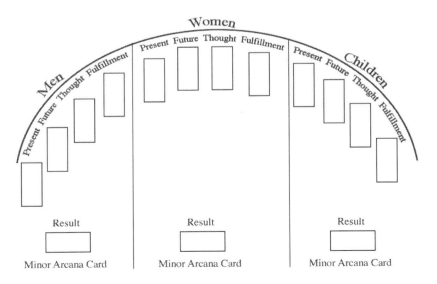

Working a Card Spread 161

I'm sorry but this chapter
is full right now.
We'll call your name when
we have an opening.

6. Other Fancy Stuff

The 6 Most Important Majors:

Things changed over time with the Tarot.
One procedure with Tarot cards has been obsolete since the 1970's.
Certain Major Arcana had more significance and influence than the rest
of the Major Arcana. There were six of them, and if they were laid next
to another card, these more powerful Majors gave the card next to it more
influence than would normally be seen.
The six Majors that had more influence were The Pope V(Hierophant),
The Wheel of Fortune X, The Devil XV, Judgment XX, The World XXI,
and The Fool XXII. *In some teachings at this time, the Fool was numbered
XXII instead of 0.*

There was no explanation given as to why these cards were supposed to be
more influential than the others.

Not Using the Complete Deck:

When I first started reading Tarot cards it was not uncommon to see readers only using the Major Arcana cards or only using the Minor Arcana
cards. Not the complete deck. Today most readers use the complete 78
card deck. I mention this to point out that things change over time and the
way we see and use the Tarot can shift as time goes on. The applications
and our perception of the cards have not been etched in stone. They shift
over time.

The Future of the Card Reading

The mystery of the Tarot was never in the cards. It's been in their application and I feel as we look into the way a card spread is done, we are looking more into the application and not so much into the actual cards themselves. Looking at the mechanics of a card spread will open up doors of understanding using these cards that have not been explored before.

As we move forward with the Tarot we will give card spreads more freedom to be altered to fit our questions precisely. With exact points of concern we seek to find answers to. So I feel that we will be focusing more on the card spreads and how they can be used in more effective ways.

The Tarot cards are considered an oracle. Which means they answer questions. Having useful questions is an important part of the whole process.

Being able to formulate constructive aspects to each question asked will be the new talent of the future card reader. Not knowing the cards in detail. Knowing the right questions to ask and creating a card spread based on those specific aspects of a question will be key to the reader in the future.

The Kinds of Divination in 1652

Although the Tarot cards were around as early as the 1400's, it seems they were not used for divination until much later. The first records we have of divination with the Tarot cards aren't until the late 1700s. In the 1600s, any type of divination was considered a crime, but the punishment was usually light. It really wasn't considered a major crime. It was considered taking advantage of naive people who believed in fortune telling. But there was some fine print in that law. If you contacted any spirits in your readings, that was considered sorcery. And for sorcery you burned at the stake! OOPS!

Here are a list of the types of divination brought to the courts of England in the year 1652. Notice that cards are not anywhere on the list.

Aeromancy, or divining by the air.
Alectryomancy, by cocks or poultry.
Alphitomancy, by meal, flour, or bran.
Antinopomancy, by the entrails of women and children.
Arithmancy, by numbers.
Astragalomancy, by dice.
Axinomancy, by saws.
Botanomancy, by herbs.
Capnomancy, by smoke.
Carromancy, by melting of wax.
Catoxtromancy, by looking glasses.
Cattabomancy, by vessels of brass or other metals.
Cephalonomancy, by broiling of an ass's head. –   Ha Ha!!
Chartomancy, by writing in papers.
Chiromancy, by the hands.
Chrystallomancy, by glasses.
Cleromancy, by lots.
Conscinomancy, by sieves.
Crithomancy, by grain or corn.
Dactylomancy, by rings.
Demonomancy, by the suggestion of evil demons or devils.
Gastromancy, by the sound of or signs upon the belly.
Geomancy, by earth.
Gyromancy, by rounds or circles.

Hydromancy, by water.
Icthyomancy, by fishes.
Idolomancy, by idols, images, figures.
Lampadomancy, by candles and lamps.
Lecanomancy, by a basin of water.
Lithomancy, by stones.
Livanomancy, by burning of frankincense.
Logarithmancy, by logarithms.
Macharomancy, by knives or swords.
Oinomany, by wine.
Omphilomancy, by the navel.
Oniromancy, by dreams.
Onomatomancy, by names.
Onychomancy, by the nails.
Ornithomancy, by birds.
Podomancy, by the feet.
Psychomancy, by men's souls, affections, wills, religious or moral disposi-
tions.
Pyromancy, by fire.
Roadomancy, by stars.
Sciomancy, by shadows.
Spatalamancy, by skins, bones, excrements.
Stareomancy, or divining by the elements.
Sternomancy, from the breast to the belly.
Sycomancy, by figs.
Theomancy, pretending to divine by the revelation of the Spirit and by the
Scriptures or Word of God.
Theriomancy, by beasts.
Tuphramancy, by ashes.
Tyromancy, by the coagulation of cheese.
Nagomancy or necromancy, by inspecting, consulting and divining by,
with, or from the dead.

–   John Gaule, Mysmantia (1652)

Now what did I do with that ass's head!? It's probably under the couch
again.

RANDOM THOUGHTS

Sometimes you hear something and it just sticks with you. It might be from a movie or from the page of a book. Sometimes they are from your own head too. When that happens to me I usually jot them down on something and then they just get lost somewhere. So I thought I would put them here before I lose them.

Some might not make sense until you let them settle in your head awhile. Some might make you laugh. Some might make you think. Just thought I would share them here. Sorta like a brain snack. And yes, some of these thoughts have nothing to do with Tarot cards. But some do.

- Imagination is the gateway to your intuition.

- As a reader – keep your watch wound.

- Never ask a person to make a decision if their arms or legs are crossed.

- Talk at the moon – Listen to the wind – Get drunk!

- Does existence have meaning?

- I truly see you when others haven't.

- 10th position – Visualize the completed goal.

- The greatest trick the Devil ever pulled was convincing the world he didn't exist.

- There is no substitute for sugar.

- My world shattered like a dish!

- A coward dies a thousand deaths – A hero only one.

- The Tarot cards stimulate ideas. And when we see those ideas we look at the cards with amazement instead of looking at ourselves.

- Everything is impossible until someone does it.

- Some people can't count to three without getting a few of the numbers wrong.

- Be a teacher – Be a leader – And do what you love to do.

- If you own a computer you have access to over 1.5 billion people. Are there clients out there for you?

- Acquiring a skill is easier today than ever before.

- Blending what we know helps figure something we're trying to achieve.

- A Tarot card reading can trigger suggestions and ideas that pertain to a question being looked into. Sometimes these suggestions and ideas can lead to dynamic answers and solutions.

- *"First they ignore you*
  Then they laugh at you
  Then they fight you
  Then you win"
  ~ Mahatma Gandhi

- The secret to creativity is curiosity.

- Nothing great was ever created by thinking rationally.

- A new idea is nothing more than two known subjects blended together.

- Ideas are meaningless if they are not put into action.

Other Fancy Stuff   169

- I would rather have elegant failure than boring success.

- Truth is what people are willing to believe.

- There are so many different combinations between a man and a woman.

- Your life quest:
  Something to live on
  Something to live for
  Something to die for

- If you have the courage to fail…..you will win.

- The person who invented the sailing ship also invented the ship wreck.

- A wise man once said nothing.

- Effort does not guarantee outcome.

- There's more than one definition to being a good Tarot reader.

- *"Courage is grace under pressure."*
  ~ E. Hemingway

- I stumbled upon a mystery of the highest magnitude.

- E. Hemingway's 6 word story.
  "For sale. Baby shoes. Never worn."

- If you eliminate all other possibilities, what remains must be the truth.

- Are we good at connecting-the-dots or just good at collecting-the-dots.

- The biggest response you will get to a new idea is criticism.

- If you want to really get to know someone personally, don't talk.

- Ghosts were created when the first man walked in the light.

- Changing your mind is a sign of intelligence.

- You cannot will a new idea to come to you.

- Card Spread's Positions: *It is a universal tendency to fragment a question into separate parts.*

- A position in a card spread is a concept of your question.

- Today we have psychological terminology to describe the application of a Tarot card reading.

- Experts are clueless to new ideas.

- It ain't gambling unless the rent's on the line.

- Don't ask questions you don't want answers to.

- If you love people, you're supposed to let them in.

- Sometimes when you win – you lose.

- Self-mastery is the 1st step towards the conquest of fate.

- Do you care enough to fail?

- We all have questions. It's part of what it means to be human.

- Reality is for people who can't face alcohol.

- Free the Glutens!

- I should be in the Hall of Fame! When I was in school, I was always placed in the hall.

- To succeed, all's you need is looks and a whole lotta money.

- No job, no rent, no money. I'm sure glad things are back to normal.

- *"I destroy my enemies when I make them my friends."*
  ~ Abraham Lincoln

- *"I have a dream."*
  ~ Martin Luther King

- Anger is poison to the soul.

- Positions are the question – The cards are the answers.

- The simple answer is usually the correct one.

- There is no Devil – that's just God when he's drunk.

- Hello darkness, my old friend. I've come to talk with you again.

- Did Adam and Eve have navels?

- *"If you don't believe in me, believe in the work that I do."*
  ~ Jesus Christ

- *"Imagination is more important than knowledge."*
  ~ Albert Einstein

- What a caterpillar calls the end of the world....God calls a butterfly.

Does this chapter make my butt look too big?

7. Conversations with the Tarot

The cards can show many things to us if we allow them to. Visualize a conversation with one of the cards. What kind of a personality would that card have? Would you two get along well?

Visualizing a card having its own way of thinking outside of your head can bring new ideas to you as well. Making the last chapter in my books a set of conversations with the cards has become a habit.

So here's another behind the scenes talk with the way these cards really act when they're off the job.

This isn't my idea. The cards keep making me do this dammit!
I wish they would just leave me alone!

I wanted this to be a serious book!

The Emperor IV
Accomplishments?

Sitting here at my table thinking about how I got through another year. It went OK. Got some things accomplished. A number of lectures, classes and many readings for clients. I have come up with some great ideas for a few more books and now I just have to get them started. Yes, a good year. It's funny but sometimes I feel that my journey is just starting, even after this long. But I'm enjoying it just the same.

Then I hear someone say, "You enjoy going around in circles?"

I turn and see the Emperor sitting across the room looking right at me.

"Well hello."

"Hello back," he says. "I asked if you enjoy going around in circles."

"What do you mean?" I asked.

"Well you're sitting here pondering all of your wonderful accomplishments this year and I have to laugh. You haven't done anything that exceptional. You threw a few cards and made a few bucks. That some big deal to you Vincent?"

"Yeah," I answered. "I made it through another year as a Tarot reader. That's my profession."

"Profession? You're a struggling soul in an obscure enterprise my friend. A craft, not a profession. A street craft I might add. That's gonna be your legacy? Not too impressive, Vincent."

"Fancy words, 'Obscure Enterprise.' It's not an obscure enterprise. It's a unique craft and it's been around a long time. I counsel and I'm good at what I do. I'm one of the best!" I said.

"Oh? So that's a big deal then? Being a card reader? Better than the rest? What have you done so different than others in your craft?"

"Well there's some people out there that feel I know the Tarot cards better than most other readers do," I said.

"So you know all about Tarot cards. You think that's all you need to do? That's like saying Stephen King became a great author by knowing all about the type of pencil he wrote his novels with. Tarot cards are just a tool Vincent. A tool for the successful reader. Are you a big name with the Tarot cards, Vincent?"

"I get by."

"You're a typical reader, that's all. No great shake."

"TYPICAL!" I yelled. "I'm far from typical pal. I feel I'm the best there is in my craft. The best! I'd put myself up against any other reader – card for card!"

"And where has that gotten you, Vincent?
Many ideas go through your head every day and you just sit on them. Manifest those ideas into a reality!
Create them. Make them real – not fantasy."

"Is that your power then?" I asked. "Turning ideas into realities?
A builder of realities?"

"Yes, that's me, Vincent."

"Well why don't you manifest my apartment getting cleaned Mr. Big Shot Emperor? Instead of telling me what I'm doing wrong."

"I wouldn't waste my time, Vincent.
I have better things to do and so should you.
Act on your ideas. Get off your butt. Although this place does look like a train wreck," he said, looking around my apartment.

"People walk around with great ideas going through their minds all the time. They just don't act on them. So what good is an idea if it just stays in your head Vincent? Turn it into a reality. People are too afraid it might fail. So they play it safe and don't do anything with their ideas or their dreams.

"Failure terrorizes people and it shouldn't. That's what makes the difference between a winner and a loser. Fear of failure. Whoever invented the sailing ship also invented the shipwreck," he said, pointing a finger at me. "Failure is all part of the game and you're in the midst of it right now. Keep on going!"

"It's easy for you to say, sure. You're the Emperor. That's what you do. Make things happen. You turn ideas into realities. I mean you are the energy behind great accomplishments. Things like the United Nations. Mathematics. Technology. Science. The compass. Even the wheel!"

"Yes, that's true," he said smugly, looking at himself in my mirror. "The wheel was really big, wasn't it?
But not everything has to be of such magnitude. There are personal accomplishments as well, Vincent."

"Well I'm trying to write another book your majesty. What do I call you anyway?"

"Your majesty sounds good to me, Vincent. I like that. And kneeling before me – looking at the floor as you speak would be kinda cool to see you do too."

"Yeah you would, Mr. Big Shot. Don't hold your breath."

He just grinned.
"I am pretty good aren't I, Vincent."

"Well how come you're not helping me then?" I asked.

"I do help you every day, Vincent. I'm that haunt inside of you that says keep going with your ideas.
That's me pestering you."

"Oh, is that what that irritating sensation in my mind is?"

"Yes. Yours truly."

"Well why don't you manifest some TV shows for me to be on? Why don't you manifest some big agent calling me on the phone right now wanting a contract with me? Huh? Mr. Big Shot Emperor? I don't hear the phone ringing, Mr. Big Shot Emperor.
See that lump of plastic over there on the coffee table? That's called a telephone. Is it ringing? No!"

"What, you want me to hold your hand through the whole thing? Hand it to you on a silver platter?" he said with a smile.

"If I did that you wouldn't feel the gratification of accomplishment. You need to manifest that yourself. It's up to you to take the initiative my friend. Network. Get out there and let people know who you are. Interaction is key, Vincent. I just plant the seeds in your mind."

"Yeah well you plant a lot of weeds in my mind too.
Why don't you plant some money in my wallet while your so busy planting."

"OOOHHHH. Poor wittle vincy wincy is twying to whyte his wittle boook."

Conversations with the Tarot 179

"*Papus* wrote *Tarot of the Bohemians* in 1889. He didn't have access to information that you have today. Same with *Levi, Case, Waite, Crowley* and the rest, Vincent. They didn't even have cars to get around in.

"They didn't have the internet to find information with. You want perks? They had to saddle a horse just to get to the library. Living in this time in history you have all sorts of perks around you. If an opportunity knocked on your door and said 'Hello, I'm an opportunity,' you would say NOT INTERESTED and slam the door in it's face!"

"Besides. I give you some perks here and there. A corporate party, new clients. Even helped get you started with your books."

"You had nothing to do with my books," I said.

"Are you sure about that, Vincent? I create opportunities don't I?"

"Well yeah, I guess so."

"It's up to you to grab them when they come. If you're bright enough, that is."

"I'm bright enough! You think you're some big deal, Mr. Emperor. Well I don't need you!"

"Show me, Vincent!"

"I'll show you alright! They'll be naming a street after me when I'm done!"

"Now your talking, Vincent!
Show me and I might even be tempted to throw some more perks your way. If I feel it's promising, that is."

"This year's gonna be spectacular! YOU WATCH ME PAL!"

"I will be. You can bet on that." he answered.

"Now I've got work to do. I can't be sitting here wasting my time talking to you, Mr. Big Shot Emperor."

"Good. We will see. And I'll be watching," he said as he walked out my door.

I closed the door behind him and thought... "I've got important things to do around here. Like how am I gonna market this book? I'll get the break I'm looking for and I'll be ready for it when it comes too."

Then I hear '*rrring....rrring.....rrring.*'
Oh, that lump of plastic on the coffee table is making a noise again.
I picked up the phone and said....*"Hello?"*

Conversations with the Tarot

The Hanged Man XII
Conformity

Conversations with the Tarot   183

Planning on having guests over for dinner tonight. I'm very excited about it all. As I plan the evening I hear a voice from behind saying "So what you gonna have?"

I turn and see the Hanged Man sitting in one of my dining room chairs. "Well hello." I said

"Hi Vincent. Thought I might come by and help out. Mind if I....hang around?" He said with a grin.

"Thanks but I've got it all figured out."

"I see we think the same." he said looking round my place

"Whaddya mean?" I said

"Well reversal of ideas. That's what I stand for. Right? Reversal. And most people don't like that concept. It's uncomfortable to them. Hence the Hanged Man seems wrong doesn't it?"

"True" I answered "Kinda topsy turvy."

"People get freaked out if things aren't like they're used to. Your guests might not like this Vincent. Look at your dinner table. A 6' folding table that you normally keep folded up against the wall. Isn't that different? Most people have some expensive dining room table that stays in place all year long. In a room that is never used for anything but dining on a few special holidays each year.

"And how about these fancy chairs of yours? OOHH patio furniture chairs. Nice idea Vincent!" he says as he looks down at the chair he's seated in.

"Yes it amazes me that more people don't use them. They only use these type of chairs to sit outside. Never inside the house. oohh no!!! That would be so wrong to do!" I answered.

"But they make so much more sense than big clunky wooden chairs. A nice set of six light weight patio chairs makes so much more sense to me. And you can stack them together and put them out of the way when your not using them." I said, putting the rest of the chairs in place.

"You and I think the same Vincent. That's why people see us as different than the rest of the world. We don't really fit in to the norm. Isn't that frustrating sometimes?" he asked.

"Sure it is, but that's their business, not mine" I said as I placed the dishes on the table for six."

"Are those dog dishes Vincent?"

"Why yes." I answered rather proudly. Showing him one of the chrome bowls. "I got'em at PETCO. Nice light weight chrome colored dog dishes. They don't tip and they don't break either. Great dishes. Dogs have better culinary than humans do.
Nothin like a good dog dish and a wooden spoon to eat beef stew from."

"Is that the main course tonight Vincent? Beef stew?"

"Yes, my superb beef stew recipe. Been in the crock pot since 5am this morning. Dinner served at 5pm this afternoon. Beef stew with my home-made corn bread."

"Some of your guests might be offended when they see you expect them to eat out of a dog dish Vincent."

"Well they were never used by a dog. I bought them brand new specifically for me."

"Might not make a difference Vincent. Remember you and I don't think like most others. New ideas aren't usually taken very well.
Have your guests been here before?"

"No, This is a first." I said.
"And these dishes work better than human dishes do. Dogs must be laughing at us when they see us eat out of those stupid, heavy, clumsy, breakable, ceramic bowls people use. They tip so easily!"

"There, the table is set nicely." I say as I look at the six placed chrome dog dishes laid out on the folding table with a nice wooden spoon at each one. And six white patio furniture chairs in place. "PERFECT! – I hope everyone comes hungry. We're gonna have a nice dinner and then we're gonna watch the game on TV. Starts at 6pm!"

"Serving any dessert?"

"Yes. Ice cream will be served as we watch the game."

"Where's the bowls for the ice cream?" he asked

"Oh yes. Almost forgot.
Here they are." I said as I place a plastic coffee mug at each setting.

"Coffee mugs! For ice cream!!??? Great idea Vince!"

"I agree! Better than a bowl. Insulated plastic coffee mugs keep the ice cream cold and you have a handle on them to hold the ice cream in instead of balancing a bowl in one hand while trying to eat the ice cream with the other. Coffee mugs works better."

"Where's the TV?"

"In the other room." I said

He looks in the other room and sees the TV but no where to sit.
"Where they gonna sit?" he asked.

"They can bring their patio chair with them into the TV room and sit where ever they like. Those chairs hardly weigh anything."

"Vincent, try to remember that most people don't see things the way you do, whether it makes sense or not, it is the way it is. Sometimes your perception of things might seem upside down but in reality might really make more sense."

"Like you, the Hanged Man, number 12 right?" I asked
"Hey, what should I call you anyway? I mean besides 'The Hanged Man."

"You can call me Darwin, DaVinci, Galileo, Tesla, Edison, Ford"

"OK – OK. I get it.
You said we're a lot alike.
So are you implying I have something in common with great minds like that?" I asked.

"Ha!" He laughed. "Only in a very small way my friend. But yes the same patterns are there. It's not that uncommon really. What you have going for you is you don't care that you're different. You don't try to be what you're not. You are you and that's that. And that's a good thing my friend."

"So the Hanged Man card can mean just thinking differently than others?" I asked.

"Sure it can Vincent. It can mean seeing things from a different perspective than the norm. And sometimes that is what is needed for great things to happen. Sometimes you may face ridicule for being different. But if the alternative means not being yourself, isn't a little ridicule worth it? So sing when standing in line at the check-out counter. Dance down the street if you like. People will like to see someone just being themselves and not caring what others think of them."

Then I hear "DING-DONG."

"Oh! It's Five 0'Clock and my guests are here!!"

I open the front door and greet them all standing there together.

"Hiiiii!!!! Come on in!" Hugs and handshakes are exchanged.
"Have a seat in the dining room. Make yourselves comfortable. I'll be right in there. Hope you like beef stew." I said as I walked into the kitchen to get the crock pot.

The Hermit IX
We know there's a mole

Sitting here late at night wondering what I can write about the Hermit, number 9.
That card can stand for hidden knowledge. Answers that need to be found. I always liked this card. The Hermit just seems so isolated and full of hidden wisdom.

That's when the phone rings. Who would be calling me this late at night! I pick up my phone and say "Hello?"

A low voice on the other end says "We need to talk.....I'll be at your place in 5 minutes" *Click*.

"WHAT! Who's coming over here now! It's after midnight! Some kook?! It must be a wrong number." I went back to my computer and continued writing.

Soon I hear footsteps coming down the hallway. "Someone's coming home late?" I thought to myself.
The footsteps stop outside my door and I hear a soft "*knock....knock... knock*" on my door.

What?!! Who could that be?

I open my door and the Hermit is standing there in his long cowl robe. He walks in uninvited. As he looks around my room he sets his lantern down on my desk and closes my drapes. Then he says "Kill the lights"

"What if I just turn them down? What's this all about?" I asked as I lowered the lights.

"You seem to be getting a lot of sensitive information about us Vincent. Who's your connection?" he says as he grabs my phone and takes out the battery.

Hey that's my phone!

"Affirmative" he says...."It might be bugged."

We know there's a mole Vincent. Who are you working for?"

"A mole? Whaddya mean a mole?" I asked

"A rat Vincent!" he answered

"A rat and a mole? Here? Any farm animals?" I answered
"Maybe a cow?"

"Don't be funny." he answered
"Where are you getting your information from? Who you workin for? The *Angel Cards* perhaps? We need to know now before it's too late." he said looking at me sternly.

"I don't know what you're talking about." I answered.

"I have all night Vincent.... Tell me, how do you explain these documents?" he says as he tosses both of my books on the table.

"Those are my books" I answered

"Ah! – So you admit it then!"

"Yeah, My name and picture are printed on the backs. See?? showing him the covers.

"Don't be coy Vincent. Who's the mole? Our sources think the *Angel cards* are behind this. – We can do this the easy way or we can do this the hard way" he says. Then he hits me in the shin with his staff a few times.

whack whack

"Hey! Cut that out!" Crazy guy comes in here, hitting me on the shin with a stick.

"We have quite a large file on you Vincent Pitiscki" he said as he pulls out a folder from his robe.

Uh...the name is PITISCI not PITISCKI" I said. Rubbing my shin bone.

"Oh, thanks. I'll make a note of that." as he erases the K on his paper.

"Vincent we can't allow you to continue with your work. You are destroying the very essence of what we are." he says as he peeks out of my drapes making sure he wasn't followed.

"Whaddya mean destroying?" I asked
"I thought I was helping"

"For centuries we've been able to keep the Tarot's mysterious knack of accurate predictions a secret. Occultist names like *PAPUS, WAITE, CROWLEY, CASE, LEVI* and many more searched, yes! But we stopped them and we'll stop you too Vincent."

"Who are you? A common card reader who just happens to stumble on our secret? We find that hard to believe Vincent. Who is your connection. Who's your contact. Is it the *Ten of Wands*? He's been acting strange lately."

"You are trying to expose our deepest secret. And that mystery is what makes the Tarot so curious to people. Its mysterious and unexplainable ability to predict the future Vincent! Which is the only reason people are intrigued by us. If your work leaks out, it will destroy us. We can't let that happen Vincent. We can't allow you to reveal that centuries old mystery!"

"Whaddya gonna do? Hit me with your stick again?" Ha!

He whacks my shin again....*whack whack*

"Hey! Cut that out!" I said as I grab the stick from his hand. "Hey...this thing is just hollow molded plastic. What you gonna do?... Annoy me to death with a plastic toy stick!" Ha!

"Well I'll admit we're not very good at 'strong arm' tactics. We never had to go this far before. I was hoping playing *Good Card – Bad Card* would get you to cooperate." he said

"But there is only one of you here" I said.

"I was multi-tasking." he said

"Look don't worry. I'm not out to destroy the Tarot. But if people can understand why it works can you imagine the improvements that could be made in doing readings with you guys?" I said

"No, I can't Vincent. Are there any?" He replied with a curious look.

"Yes! Lots of improvements can be made once the application is seen for what it is. Explaining why it works opens up new doors of understanding. Trust me, the Tarot will be better off for it. There's no mole telling me your secrets. Today we know more than we did when the Tarot first came around. It's a great method to find answers and it works. Now it can be shown why it works with clear conclusive facts based on psychological research and study. It's a new age my friend." I explained

"So the Tarot will benefit from taking the mystery out of it?" he said

"Of course it will. Because it opens up new doors of mystery. The mystery of the mind and using its wonderful capabilities." I replied

"Better than before? No more scepticism! No more bad mouthing what we are as a silly fantasy. We would be a legitimate source of ideas?" he said, looking at me with surprise.

"Yeah – That's right!!" I said

"Well, wait till the others hear about this! We'll have a celebration for sure! You're taking us out of the darkness Vincent!
Is your shin OK? Sorry about that." he said with concern.

"Yes, it's fine I said as I rubbed my leg. Molded plastic staff huh? Like a *whiffle* staff? Ha! Well, it looks very realistic." I said handing it back to him.

"Look it – You know I love all you guys. I've had you around for many years. Actually I don't know what I would do without you."

"Really Vincent?"

"Really Hermit." I said

"So there's no mole? And this getting leaked out to the public won't destroy interest in the Tarot?" he asked.

"Nah! It will make it even better. We know more about the mind and how to use it today. Imagine the possibilities this could bring if people really understood why the Tarot works. They would be able to improve on it. Make it more proficient. And learn to read in ways never done before. Better ways. That's why I write books about the Tarot.

If you understand how something works you can improve on it. You guys will be better than ever. All 78 of you. Trust me."

"Vince, you're the best. I wish you were one of us. A new Tarot card added to the family. The Vince card!"

Ha! " If you added me into the Tarot – what would I represent?" I asked

I dunno. We'd figure something out for you. Maybe 'Vince-ness.' *A time to focus on 'vince-ness'* he replied thinking out loud.

"Wha? What's *vince-ness*?" – I asked.

"I dunno. We would work out those details later on" he said

"Well thanks but I like the relationship as it stands right now. No need to change it. Besides, I don't think anyone is trying to attain *'vince-ness'* in their lives"

"Ah, maybe you're right. So we're cool Vince?" he asked

"Yes, we're fine Hermit."

With that he smiled, shook my hand and walked out.

As he closed the door behind him, I sat thinking about what's just happened. Then I noticed the lantern still sitting on my desk. Oh well, I guess he'll be back. Nice lantern.

Hey! I wonder if this thing's bugged!

The Sun XIX
Appreciated

Conversations with the Tarot   197

Thought it was time to write about the Sun card of the Major Arcana. As I sit there wondering, I think to myself...Is it hot in here or what. Maybe I'll open a window; turn on the fan.

Then I hear someone say "Hello sunshine."

I look behind me and see a big bright yellow face wearing sunglasses floating there in the room! Wow!

"Are you the Sun???!!!"

"In the flesh Vincent– Or maybe I should say...In the *'hydrogen, oxygen, carbon, nitrogen, magnesium, iron and a little silicon."*

I just stared trying to shield my eyes from the brightness. "Can you turn that down a little. You're hurting my eyes."

"Sure Vincent, how's this? " he said as the room dimmed to a nice level.

"A lot better, Thanks. Hey I'm happy to meet you." I said

"Yes, I do have a tendency to brighten up people's days don't I? I'm glad you're writing about me Vincent. This is exciting!" he replied

"Really? Writing a couple of pages in a book about you excites you?" I said

"You're the SUN. You've been recognized by mankind throughout history. Even worshiped!"

"Ah yes, the good ol days.
But no one really talks to me anymore. It's just like...OK....the sun is out. I don't get as much attention as I used to get. They're too busy to be think- ing about me today. People need to get outside more. No one thinks I'm a big deal anymore. So this conversation is a nice change."

"Well I'm glad to hear it. What should I call you anyway?"

"The Sun." he said with a blank look.

"Oh, well yeah, I guess that would work." I said.

"Did you know that I was your first god?" he asked
I mean even before Shiva, Budha, Jesus, Isis, well all of them."

"Yeah I guess you were."

"I mean I am life giving. And I am the light. I give you warmth, breath, things that grow for you to eat. I protect you against the darkness. And it's very rewarding to me too. "

"It is?"

"Yes."

"Well you're a hot item that's for sure." Ha!

"Yes, about 30 million degrees F. Give or take." said the Sun

"Wow, that's hot!"

Yes, but it's a dry heat Vincent."

Hey, if you're that hot how come those sunglasses you're wearing aren't melting."

"Are you kidding Vincent? These are *RayBans*. They're too cool to melt."

"Hey, are you God?" I asked

"Well lets just say you will understand more as time goes on my friend."

"uh-huh, OK."

"Well I think you are what we perceive as God."

He smiles a big grin.
"They even named glasses after me."

"They did?"

"Sure....SUN..glasses!
And all your movie stars wear them."

"So, when I come up in those Tarot cards what do you think it means Vincent?"

"Well always good news." I said.
"Nurturing situation, bright future, things seen clearly. New life on a goal. Centering on issues of concern."

"Well Vincent, how about many opportunities all around you hidden in plain sight. Answers that are so close to you that you don't see them. You live in a perfect environment and I am all around you. Everywhere you look, Even at night, I'm close by. Life giving that is so vital you can't imagine being without it. Things kept in order, a good foundation, planned movement, cycles, one of many." said the Sun

"How do you mean one of many?" I asked

"Come on Vincent. Carl Sagan? Billions and billions– remember?"

"Oh yeah. Carl Sagan. He was one of your biggest fans."

"But I do like your idea of centering too Vincent."

"Well if it weren't for you all the planets, including Mother Earth here would just fly out into deep space. Right? No centering?" I said.

"Yes, and its a little chilly out there in deep space Vincent."

"How chilly?" I asked

"About 450 degrees below zero Vincent.
So if you decide to go outside of my area you better bundle up."

"I'm not planning leaving anytime soon." I said.

"Me either." said the Sun.

"Good. We need you here. You can come by anytime." I said

"Good. I'll see you tomorrow."

"I hope so." I said as he faded away.

The Lovers VI
Ain't dat right darlin?

Conversations with the Tarot 203

Out in my hallway I hear a man and woman having a conversation.

"This is a bad idea"

"No it's not. Be quiet"

"I think you're wrong but then again what else is new."

"I'm not wrong and shut up will ya. For pete sake Hubie will ya comb your damn hair please. He's gonna think you're a slob or somethin."

"I'm not a slob! I'm comfortable. Is that a crime?"

"Oh so the slob is comfortable. Well at least your comfortable....slob!"

"Oh– and you're an oil painting? Look in the mirror will ya."

"Schh! This is it! His apartment. Knock on the door."

"You knock on the door. You're the one who wanted to come here."

"Schhhh." *Knock Knock...Knock Knock*

Damn! "WHO'S THERE?" I yell through the door.

— *Knock Knock...Knock Knock*

"Ok Ok" I said as I open the door. I see an old couple standing there. A short stocky old woman with curly gray hair wearing blue jeans, sneakers and a white tee shirt and a tall skinny old guy with wispy white hair wearing an old pair of black khakis, work shoes and a wrinkled, striped shirt, buttoned crooked so that the right side is higher than the left by two buttons.

I say "Hello–Can I help you?"

"Yeah" she says as she walks in and looks around my room. He follows and says "hi".

Then she says "See? What did I tell ya? I told ya didn't I? See?"

He just nods in agreement and I say "What? Who are you two? and what you doing in my place?"

She looks at him and says "See? He doesn't know who we is. I told you he wouldn't know."

"Know what?" I said "Who the hell are you guys!"

"Come on Vince. Guess. Come on." she says.

"I don't know you." I answered.

"Need a hint?" she says as she rests her head on his shoulder and bats her eyes showing a big grin. He just stands there looking bored as he looks around my room.

"I need you two to get outta here!"

"See Hubie Hon?, I told you he wouldn't know who we was.
He's no Tarot card reader." She says, resting her head on his shoulder.

Conversations with the Tarot 205

"Wait a minute! Who comes into my place and says I don't know the cards!"

"Sandy that's who" she says with a smile showing a few crooked teeth.

"He doesn't know those tarot cards Hubie hon."
He just laughs and as he grins his false teeth drop a little outta place.

"Who are you two!"

"We's the Lovers Vince! The Lovvveeeers.
Ain't dat right Hubie honey?" she says as she puts her arm around his waist and gives him a squeeze.

"What!!! The Lovers!! You mean like from the Tarot cards Lovers?!!!"

"That's right Vince..That is us." she says.

"You mean number Six....of the Major Arcana...The Lovers....."

"He seems surprised Hubie hon."

"He just grins and laughs some more as he nods his head looking around my room."

"But you can't be the Lovers!! You two are really old...and really ug–.....
You two are really old."

"That's right Vince, we is really old and we still loves each other too.
Ain't dat right Hubie darlin?"

"uuuu yeah", he mumbles out a small laugh as he nods his head.

"But the lovers are young!"

"Not always Vince. You can still be in love when you is old too Vince. Ain't dat right Hubie?"

"eh yeah. When are we going for chinese?" he said "You said we were just gonna stop for a minute. It's way past a minute. Let's go. OK?." he continued

"Will ya shut up Hube! We just got here for chriss sake."

"I'm hungry, lets get chinese like we said we would."

"Hubie does your brain work at all? All morning that's all you think of is eating chinese. You get the same damn thing every time. Egg Fu Yung."

"Vince that's all he ever gets every time we go eat chinese. Egg Fu Yung."

"Hubie. Wanna try some pot stickers?
No...I want Egg Fu Yung."

"What's a matter with Egg Fu Yung?" he asked

"He has no brains Vince."

"I got brains. You don't have any brains." he said.

"Where you keep your brains Hubie? In your butt? They ain't in your head, that's for sure. Take your brains out of your butt and put them back in your head where they belong Hubie."

"Oh the profound scientist has spoken" he says

"Why do I put up with this Vince?" Ya know when I was young, I coulda married a doctor. His name was Frank. And he was so cute too. But I decided to marry Mr. Egg Fu Yung eating genius here instead."

"I think that doctor's name was Frankenstein, not Frank. And he created you. Ha Ha" he said.

Conversations with the Tarot   207

"You see what I have to put up with Vince? A brainless egg fu young eating butt head. Vince his brain never matured to full size."

"Oh, the mummy speaks!" he said

"OK, I need you two to settle down." I said

"You see what you started Hubie? You got Vince all upset. You're so ignorant. He's just ignorant Vince. He can't help it."

"Well you're the one who wanted to barge in and bother this guy. Just like you bother everyone else you come in contact with." he said

"How do I bother anyone?"

"You open your big mouth. That's how you bother everyone. You open up your big mouth and suck all the oxygen out of the room every time you speak with your big mouth."

"OK, you two just settle down for a minute will ya?
You two are supposed to be the lovers right? Old ones but the lovers just the same. How long have you two been together?" I asked

"Long time." she says and he just nods in agreement.

"I want to tell you both I appreciate you coming by and helping me with the Lovers Tarot card. You two have seen much of life together and have faced it all side by side for many years. That's something to be proud of. Nothing to do with wealth or living fancy. It's just living it out together and you two did that. Two souls that decided to go through this thing we call life – hand in hand."

They both look in opposite directions from each other in silence.

"Be proud of your bond together. Now give each other a hug OK?"

She and he both turn to each other. He looks down at her and she peeks up at him.

"Come on you two. Make up." I said

Then she says "I'm sorry Hubie."

He says "I'm sorry Sandy" Then he kisses her on the check and she hugs him close to her and rests her head on his chest.

"There! I'm glad to see the Lovers back on track here."

"Now why don't you two go out and get some Chinese food. Egg Fu Yung sound good Hube?" I asked

"Yeah." he says

I open my door and say "Thanks for the visit. See ya. Bye."

As they walk down the hall I hear her say. "I'm gonna order some pot stickers. You wanna try a pot sticker Hubie?"

"Naw, ...Egg Fu Young for me."

"OK – Just a thought." she says.

"Dat Vincent was a nice man Hubie." she says

"Yeah I guess." he says

Conversations with the Tarot

Temperance XIV
Inspiration?

Conversations with the Tarot   211

```
I've always had a difficult time understanding the
Temperance card-number 14.
```

"What to write here....What does that card mean –really. The image on that card is not really saying anything. She's just standing there pouring water from one urn to another. I always tell people that the Temperance card represents inspiration. Angels are here to inspire us. They have the power to help guide us on finding our passion."

Then I hear a voice say "I like that Vincent –That's good!
So have I inspired you then?"

I turn around in my chair and the Temperance angel is standing right behind me.

"WOW! Temperance! Hi!"

"Thought I would help out.
You're just staring at that screen so I felt you could use a spark."

"Well thanks."

"So you want that book you're writing to be successful don't you?"

"Yeah, I guess, yeah I do."

"Well you got a long way to go Vincent."

"But I think the book is coming along. Isn't it?" I said

"It's OK, but I think you can use a little boost.
Let's try this Vincent. Who in your life inspired you? Anybody?"

"I dunno. Lotta people did, I guess."

"Who? Think of someone specific who inspired you."

"I know. The Lone Ranger! He inspired me."

"OK. That's good Vincent. Now think of yourself as the Lone Ranger only with Tarot cards. That might help."

"I can do that, yes.
Actually I think I would make a real good Lone Ranger.
I can see that yes! Wearing a mask!
With my faithful Indian companion Toto!
Yes! Get a gun too! With silver bullets! I can see me now riding into the sunset on a white horse! Yeah!"

"The Indian companion was Tonto, Vince.
You're getting carried away. I just meant who inspired you.
That's all. Like an example to motivate you forward."

"But I bet I would make a real good Lone Ranger!" I said

"Vincent...The Lone Ranger went out and captured dangerous criminals. You read Tarot cards. OK?"

"No, I really could do that though."

"Don't even think about it Vincent.
I don't need to see a 64 year old man walking down the street with a mask carrying a pistol. Your Lone Ranger career would only last a few blocks before the police threw you into the back of a squad car. OK? Just settle down."

"What? I could be the Lone Ranger if I wanted to!"

"No Vincent. You would probably hurt yourself so don't even think about it. Besides, you probably wouldn't know the difference between a horse and a giraffe. Let alone ride one. But you do have passion Vincent. And you have heart too. That much I'll give you. But you need to follow that passion Vincent. That's all I'm saying."

"I do." I said "I'm pretty good at my work aren't I?"

Conversations with the Tarot 213

"You need more than just being good at something to be successful." she continued. "That's only a small part of success."

"It is? Well what am I missing then." I asked.

"You need to develop a strong interactive relationship with your following."

"What following? How do I do that?" I said

"You've stumbled upon something that is remarkable. In other words, something worth remarking about. You have found a way to explain in a logical and rational way why the centuries old Tarot has been such an amazing method to predict the future.

And when people see that, it will attract those who are listening. Create an interest that others of your profession can become a part of. Being sincere about it helps tremendously too. And you are sincere, I'll give you that." She said as she patted me on the shoulder.

"Figure out what people really want with the Tarot and give it to them. You know enough about the Tarot to do that Vincent."

"OK, well I'm already doing those things, aren't I? I'm sincere and I teach and write about it, right? How come it's still not hitting home then?" I asked

"You're not getting across to them. You're still blending in with the rest of the Tarot world. Everyone wants to blend in. Everyone wants to be right in the middle of it all and not stand out from the crowd. Everyone wants to be more average than average.

That's not too inspiring Vincent. Look at the kids today. Getting a college degree with high grades. That's their goal. So now we have everyone with a college degree and high grades and just blending right in with all the others who have college degrees and high grades. You become average. You become the norm. It's so sad to see everyone wanting to be a perfect cog in the wheel of life."

"So being sincere and having something remarkable gets you out of that rut then?" I asked

"Well, no. There's more." she continued

"OK...what?" I asked as I drank my coffee.

"Stand out from the crowd. You're an artist. You're a genius. You all are geniuses. You just talk yourselves out of being that way. If what you create is unique and remarkable you will go far. You're just not taught how to do that. But if you follow what inspires you it will come naturally to you."

"Is that what you represent then? Inspiration?" I said

"I represent that flame in everyone. That passion that comes from the spirit within you. That is unshakable once you find it Vincent."

"But you're usually just seen as an angel pouring water from one urn to another. Many get confused with your real meaning."

"I give you inspiration Vincent. That is my gift to you. That is what living your life is all about. Finding what moves your soul. That is what I'm here to guide you to find. Your passion. That's what keeps you alive. And I guide you on that path. Your guardian angel."

"What?! You're my guardian angel?!"

"Well of course I am. I'm here aren't I?"

"Well where the hell have you been all this time?!"

"I'm 64 years old. About time you got here! My luck, I get a slacker guardian angel!"

"You haven't made my job easy Vincent. Actually I will probably get promoted after taking on this job."

Conversations with the Tarot   215

"Manage your passion well, whether you teach the cards, read the cards, or write about them. Manage it well. Have others walk away from you with something valuable gained from the experience."

"And lead. Leading your following is important too.
Help them find what they seek."

"That's up to them isn't it?" I said.

"Not if you are a leader it isn't.
Show them how to do what they seek to do most.
You take that initiative. That's a leader. Set them on their path. Show them their options. That creates a following. Taking action. The knights in the Tarot deck stand for action. Be a knight. Take them somewhere on their quest. Lead them."

"But you need to inspire them too." she continued. "Inspiration can come from anywhere in the mix of things. It doesn't have to come from me up here at the top. It can come from regular people like yourself.

Keep them interested and enthused about where they're heading and what they're doing. Show them their strengths and bring out their unique talents. Show them that being different has more value than blending in with the others. Show them that breaking away from the norm won't be the end of their world. It's the beginning!"

She poured more coffee into my cup from her urn and said "Good grades and a college degree are wonderful accomplishments to be proud of. But remember that all of you have unique qualities that sets you apart from the rest. And that is where your real value lies. Your individuality. What makes you –you? Your passion does that."

"Follow your passion Vincent. Act on things that move you. Finding a place where your uniqueness is sought and your passion is wanted. That is your quest in life. A knight's search for a quest." she said as she tossed the Knight of Cups from my deck down in front of me.

"You need to have a deep knowledge about your field in order to do that though. You already have that Vincent. You know those cards well enough. You are a Tarot geek Vincent! Hell you even know why they work. That makes you a leader right there. No one else sees that, do they? But you do. "

I just sat there listening trying to absorb it all as I drank my coffee.

"You know more about the Tarot than most and you also broke open the biggest mystery of the Tarot. Why they work! With that breakthrough using the Tarot can now be a hundred times more effective than ever before. Now it can be improved, renovated, advanced. Because now people can understand why they work. It's no longer a mystery thanks to you. And you my friend, are the only one who ever saw it. You saw it because it was your true passion. So lead the way."

"Well thanks for seeing my talent. Coming from you that means something." I said

"What you are really doing is following your passion. That's the key. Not talent. Passion. Talent doesn't go very far without passion behind it. Passion is what makes you stand up and make it happen. Are you ready to act? If not, you don't have the passion. And the time to act is always right now. It's always been right in front of you. Just reach for it Vincent."

"I take some action here and there. I know what I'm doing. I'll be fine."

"No you don't. I see you and you're a slacker. You play things by ear all the time. You don't prepare anything. Not even your talks. You just go out there and start blabbing. Look at me – I'm talking. *Blab – Blab – Blab*. That doesn't work Vincent. You need to grab their interest. You can do that Vincent."

"Just grab it...it's right there in front of you. It would be so easy. Quit teasing yourself. Just reach a little bit further. It's that simple. My job is to just get you to see that. Then when you do, I'll be gone. Just...Like...That. POOF!"

When I blinked, the room was empty. Wow. I guess I was just day dreaming again. Better get back to my book. Where was I. Oh yes,
Writing about the Temperance card.

```
I've always had a difficult time understanding the
Temperance card-number 14.
```

That's right – I just finished the book.
I highly recommend getting it.
Radical Tarot – Breaking all the Rules
by some guy. Just go to Amazon.

ABOUT THE AUTHOR

Vincent Pitisci has been involved with the Tarot cards since 1969.
He has made it his livelihood since 1992. He also teaches the Tarot privately as well as group classes in the Chicago area.

Vincent and his life partner Lynda Spino have been working together as intuitives' since 1993 and live in Chicago's SW suburbs of Berwyn,IL

More information can be found on him on the internet.

Pitisci's other books:
Genius of the Tarot – A Guide to Divination with the Tarot
The Essential Tarot – Unlocking the Mystery
Stray Tarot – How to Survive as a Tarot Reader

All are available on Amazon and Barnes and Nobel.

Printed in Poland
by Amazon Fulfillment
Poland Sp. z o.o., Wrocław